CREATE COMPUTER GAMES — DESIGN AND BUILD YOUR OWN GAME

by Patrick McCabe

WILEY

Published by: **John Wiley & Sons, Inc.**, 111 River Street, Hoboken, NJ 07030-5774, www.wiley.com

Copyright © 2018 by John Wiley & Sons, Inc., Hoboken, New Jersey

Published simultaneously in Canada

For general information on our other products and services, please contact our Customer Care Department within the U.S. at 877-762-2974, outside the U.S. at 317-572-3993, or fax 317-572-4002. For technical support, please visit https://hub.wiley.com/community/support/dummies.

Wiley publishes in a variety of print and electronic formats and by print-on-demand. Some material included with standard print versions of this book may not be included in e-books or in print-on-demand. If this book refers to media such as a CD or DVD that is not included in the version you purchased, you may download this material at http://booksupport.wiley.com. For more information about Wiley products, visit www.wiley.com.

Library of Congress Control Number: 2017959162

ISBN: 978-1-119-40418-7 (pbk); ISBN: 978-1-119-40422-4 (ebk); ISBN: 978-1-119-40424-8 (ebk)

Manufactured in the United States of America

10 9 8 7 6 5 4 3 2 1

CONTENTS

INTRODUCTION

This book explains the basics of game design using the free game development tool Unity. This book was created to make Unity accessible for young adults who are interested in the process of game design but don't know where to begin.

Game design is tough. It involves figuring out and understanding everything from design to coding. Knowing where to begin is daunting and can feel inaccessible. Just keep in mind that no one starts off great at game design. You don't need to know everything to start, and thinking that you do is one of the hardest challenges to overcome.

This book was written to get people like me to start thinking about game design in a different way. This book isn't about making a perfect game or about teaching you everything about game development or even Unity. This book is a starting line. It teaches the basics and encourages you to think about games differently.

ABOUT THIS BOOK

This book was written with the thought that games are tough to make and that coding is confusing. Think of this like a cookbook that explains why you use two eggs instead of three and what the pepper does to help bring out the flavor. The codes and game development that this book walks you through are approached from the bottom up. Things make sense when you understood *why* certain codes or components are needed. Just knowing the ingredients to a recipe doesn't teach you how to cook.

FOOLISH ASSUMPTIONS

This book was written for teenagers who have an interest in developing games. People who have spent years working in game design will find this book repetitive and probably not useful at all. I don't pretend that this teaches everything about game design — I know for a fact that it doesn't. This book is an introduction to the field, so it was made for people who have little to no idea where to even begin when they design their games. Some rudimentary typing skills and access to a computer and the Internet are all you really need to read this book. You'll also need a copy of Unity, which you can download for free (I'll show you how).

ICONS USED IN THIS BOOK

Throughout this book, I use the following icons:

 Tips give some clarifications or offer shortcuts. I use tips to help you understand the program better or do things in an easier way.

 Anything marked by the Remember icon reminds you of principles or ideas that you should think about through-out your game development.

WHERE TO GO FROM HERE

This book takes you step by step through the process of designing a 3D platformer. If you have a clear idea of what game development is and know about Unity's interface, you can skip the first two chapters and start with Chapter 3, where I dive into actually developing a game.

Chapters 8 through 10 use a separate program known as Blender and go into the basics of animation. If you aren't interested in adding animation or you already have animations you want to include in your game, you can skip those chapters.

All the other chapters build off of each other and are designed to take you through the steps necessary for developing an example game that you'll build with this book.

CHAPTER

01

What Is Game Design?

In this chapter, you'll ask yourself questions about not just *your* games but *all* games. When you're designing computer games, you need to think about the fundamental reasons people play games in the first place. The reasons people play strategy games aren't the same reasons they play horror games. Both kinds of games are fun, but for very different reasons. The goal of this chapter is to help you understand what those reasons are so that the games you design deliver what your players are looking for.

Understanding how game mechanics and themes work together to create a gaming experience will help you better visualize and create your own game. If the mechanics aren't fun or don't fit, it doesn't matter how cool the theme is — the game won't be fun. If the theme doesn't match the mechanics, the game might be fun but it won't be memorable. If you aim to create great games, you need to understand both mechanics and themes before you even open the software you'll use to build your games.

THINKING ABOUT WHAT MAKES FUN GAMES FUN

Have you ever played a game that you couldn't put down? One that gave you the ability to shut off your mind without a care in the world because you were just hooked on it? A game that was just a lot of fun? I'm sure you have! Otherwise, you wouldn't be reading this book.

But why were you sucked into the games you love? Why are they so addicting? What makes them fun?

Fun is where games live and die. If a game isn't fun, nobody plays it. The first thing you have to understand, though, is that there are different types of fun, and different kinds of games:

- **Fighting games** reward quick thinking and reading your opponent's moves and figuring out the proper combo to counter it with.

- **Strategy games** (like XCOM 2, shown in Figure 1-1) challenge you to think and plan for a variety of situations, sometimes in an instant.

Figure 1-1: XCOM 2.

- **Adventure games** push you to explore and discover more about the world around you.

- **Horror games** (like Slender: The Arrival, shown in Figure 1-2) get your adrenaline pumping and push your natural curiosity to its limits.

- **Puzzle games** reward you for solving different complex puzzles and for problem solving.

- **Platformers** (like Super Meat Boy, shown in Figure 1-3) work off of reward and punishment and challenge you to master the controls and the timing to perfectly execute a level.

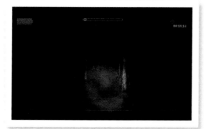

Figure 1-2: Slender: The Arrival.   Figure 1-3: Super Meat Boy.

And these are just a fraction of the types of games that are available to play. Like films, there are many different genres, some broad (like action games) or specific (like puzzle-based fighting games — look up Super Puzzle Fighter).

Whether it's to feel accomplished after beating a challenging level, or to feel powerless as you wander through the woods while an unknown monster hunts you, you want a game to provoke some sort of emotion in you. Fun comes from a game provoking the right emotion at the right time.

If you think about it, this is the same reason you watch a movie or read a book. When you want to laugh, you watch a comedy. When you want to cry, you read a tragedy. Understanding that fun comes in many different forms and goes beyond a single emotion can open up a variety of game design that you may not have thought about before.

When you're designing your game, ask yourself what type of emotion your game is trying to provoke — and capitalize on it! Sometimes that feeling is the excitement you feel in the heat of a battle. Other times, it's the sadness you feel after a game forces you to question your own mortality and life choices, like in one of my favorite games, To the Moon (see Figure 1-4).

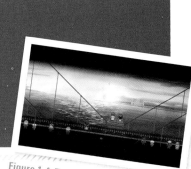

Figure 1-4: To the Moon.

ASKING THE RIGHT QUESTIONS BEFORE YOU BEGIN

REMEMBER

You don't have to answer these questions in this order. Often in game design, you start by answering any one of these questions and build out from there. There is no right or wrong order to answer these questions, but you should answer all of them before you start designing your game.

Think of game design like making something good to eat. You wouldn't just throw any ingredient into a pan and hope for the best. To make it taste great, you need to start by asking yourself what kind of food you want to make. Are you making a salad? An appetizer? A soup or dessert? Once you know what the purpose of the food is — to be a satisfying entrée or a sweet treat at the end of a meal, for example — you can choose a recipe that will get you to your goal. And after you take it out of the oven or finish combining the ingredients, you might decorate it or add a garnish to make it look good.

Similarly, before you design a game, you need to ask yourself what type of game you want to make and who will be playing the game. In this section, I've listed some of the questions you should ask yourself.

WHAT IS YOUR GAME ABOUT?

Do you want to make a war game that puts players in the middle of World War II or a game about a haunted children's restaurant where animatronic machines are trying to kill you? What your game is about can help you think about the story and help contextualize some of the

decisions you'll make as you're designing your game.

WHAT TYPE OF GAME ARE YOU MAKING?

Is your game a choice based role-
playing game (RPG) or a more linear
platformer? There are many different
types of games that you can make. The
type you choose can drastically change
how people see your game.

Figure 1-5: Five Nights at Freddy's.

Imagine if Skyrim were a 2D platformer, or if Five
Nights at Freddy's (shown in Figure 1-5) gave you
the ability to move around. Imagine how different those games would be.

> **REMEMBER**
>
> Mechanics com-
> plement story.
> Whatever type
> of game you aim
> to make, keep in
> mind how different
> mechanics can
> change the audi-
> ence for the game.

WHAT TYPE OF FEELING ARE YOU AIMING TO PROVOKE WITH YOUR GAME?

Do I want my player to feel powerful or powerless?
A game that encourages exploration in a vast
wasteland, like Fallout 4 (shown in Figure 1-6),
provokes different feelings than a game that puts
players in a cramped hallway. You want to go into
your game knowing what type of feelings you
want the player to feel. Knowing this can influence
mechanic and story decisions.

> **REMEMBER**
>
> No matter what,
> the player will feel
> *something* when she
> plays your game. And
> one way to ensure
> that she isn't bored
> when she's supposed
> to be excited is to
> make the game with
> the type of feeling
> in mind you aim to
> provoke.

WHO IS YOUR PLAYER PLAYING AS?

Is he a soldier in the war fighting for his coun-
try, or is he the civilian just trying to
survive as the war happens around
him? When you make your game, think
of how you want to frame your story
or your characters. The story of a brave
knight trying to vanquish her nemesis,
the evil warlock, is far different than a
story of an evil knight bent on defeating the good wizard.

Figure 1-6: Fallout 4.

WHAT IS THE PLAYER'S OBJECTIVE?

Games have goals. Sometimes the goal is to defeat the villain. Other times, it's to survive until morning. Think of your game as a story. Characters need a purpose. Mario isn't just running around the mushroom kingdom for fun. He's going to rescue the princess. Setting a clear objective for your player will give her direction in your game. Even games that focus on exploration set objectives that the player can strive for. Even if the objective isn't the most important part of your game, it's important to have one.

WHAT OBSTACLES WILL YOUR PLAYER FACE?

What is stopping your player from reaching his goal? Games aren't fun without any challenge. You never want your player to be bored in your game. The easiest way to prevent boredom is to understand what types of obstacles the player needs to overcome. This can take the shape of enemy characters trying to kill your player or just puzzles that the player has to solve.

WHO IS YOUR PLAYER?

The most important question of all is who you're designing your game for. The type of person who plays a peaceful game like Minecraft (shown in Figure 1-7) may not be the same type of person who plays a fast-paced fighting game like Street Fighter. Knowing the type of person you want to play your game can help determine the type of game you create.

Figure 1-7: Minecraft.

If you're ever in doubt about who your player base is, ask yourself if you would want to play the game you're making. Don't design the game you think people want to play. Design the game *you* want to play.

CREATING YOUR GAME ON PAPER

A good exercise is to create a game on paper before you go into designing a game on the computer. This will help you understand the importance of mechanics in your game without your getting caught up with all the bells and whistles that come with a theme. Try thinking of a simple objective-based game that a person can play with just a pen and paper.

REMEMBER

Paper games are tough because you need to get the player interested in the game without the fluff or theme. But in the end, if a game isn't fun, a theme — no matter how cool — won't fix it. Themes are important, but if you don't have an interesting game without the theme, no one will want to play it.

Unity: The Software You'll Use to Build Your Game

Unity is a program that you can download online for free — just go to www.unity3d.com/get-unity/download. Developed by Unity Technologies, this open-source program has opened up game development for a whole new generation of game developers (like you!). You can use Unity to develop 2D and 3D games, but for the purposes of this book, I show you how to develop a 3D game.

In this chapter, you'll learn some basic organization techniques that will help you manage your game creation. I show you how to create a new file in Unity, introduce you to the basic layouts and controls of Unity, and explain how to create an in-game object. This chapter may not be the most exciting, but you really need to understand these basics before beginning your game, so don't skip ahead!

Similar to the games you play (and will create!), game making is modular. You have to take things one step at a time. In later chapters, you'll dive into more difficult parts of game creation that have way more moving pieces and files to keep track of. Organizing your files and knowing the layout of Unity will save you the headache of trying to locate your files or tools, not to mention hours trying to retrace your steps.

GETTING ORGANIZED

Whether you're baking cookies or changing the oil in your car or developing a computer game, you need to get organized first. Getting organized isn't the fun part of any job, but it makes every job easier.

Unity does a lot of heavy lifting when it comes to organizing the files you need to create your computer game. But before you begin creating your game, you need to create a directory to store all your games in. This directory serves two purposes:

- **It creates an easy-to-remember spot on your computer for you to find all your files.** The last thing you want to have to do is dig around through a bunch of folders looking for where you saved your game.

- **Creating backups and transferring your files is much easier when they're all in the same spot.** You don't want some files in one place and other files in another. All your files for your games should be in the same area. Think of it the way you think of the notebooks you keep for your classes. You wouldn't put your biology notes in your English notebook and that history quiz in your French folder — at least not if you want to pass those classes! The same goes for the files you use to build your computer games.

REMEMBER

Computers are stupid — they can't find files if you move them. To save yourself a ton of time and frustration, store all your files in one location.

Every time you start to create a new game, make a simple directory to store your files in. Unity automatically creates simple directories for your files, but for the purposes of the game you'll be making in this book, you also need a directory that will include files outside the ones that Unity uses. To create a directory, follow these steps:

1. Create a folder called `Unity_Games` in the `My Documents` folder on your computer.

2. Inside the `Unity_Games` folder, create a folder called `Boxo_3D_Platformer`.

3. Inside the `Boxo_3D_Platformer` folder, create two folders called `Blender_Files` and `Unity_Files`.

When you create games on your own, apart from this book, you can make these directories as specific or as broad as you want, to include things like music files, sound files, image files, and so on. For the purposes of the game you're building in this book, the directory described here (shown in Figure 2-1) will serve you just fine.

Figure 2-1: The directory for your new game.

CREATING A NEW FILE

When you have your directory set up (see the preceding section), you're ready to create a new file. Follow these steps:

1. **Open Unity.**

2. **Click Create a New File.**

   The new project screen appears (see Figure 2-2).

Figure 2-2: The New Project screen.

3. **In the Project Name field, enter** Boxo_3D_Platformer.

4. **In the Location field, enter** Unity_Files.

   That's the folder you create in the preceding section.

5. **Select the 3D button.**

6. **Click Create Project.**

   A new folder is created within the Unity_Files folder that contains all your game information, as well as all your *assets* (components that are used within the game, game objects, characters, music, images, and other types of files used in our game are all examples of assets).

UNDERSTANDING HOW UNITY IS LAID OUT

When you open Unity, you're greeted with a scary-looking screen (shown in Figure 2-3). *Do not be scared of Unity.* The best way to get over your natural fear is to understand what every part of the screen is and how it relates to the game you're creating.

Scene window   Toolbar

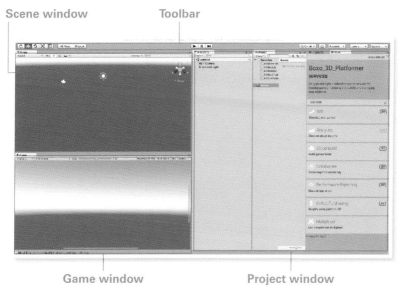

Game window   Project window

Figure 2-3: This is what you see when you open Unity.

Here's what you're looking at in Figure 2-3:

- **Scene window:**   The Scene window, one of the two main windows in Unity, is where you place and set up your game objects.

Game objects include everything that helps visualize your game. This includes objects that the player sees within the game, such as 3D objects and game text, as well as aspects of the scene that help bring the scene to life, such as lights and cameras.

- **Game window:**   The Game window, the other main window in Unity, gives you a sense of how your game will look like when you finish. It's a preview that lets you see what adjustments you need to make.

- **Project window:**   The Project window allows you to manage the assets of your project. It organizes files by type. In the upper-right corner of the Project window, you can search for specific assets. Later on, the Project window will allow you to access your materials, scenes, prefabs, scripts, and other assets.

- **Toolbar:** The Toolbar (shown in greater detail in Figure 2-4) is located at the top of the screen. It gives you control over the scene, allowing you to transform the objects and move around the entire scene area. On the Toolbar, you find the controls for playing and pausing the game and accessing your account on the Unity cloud.

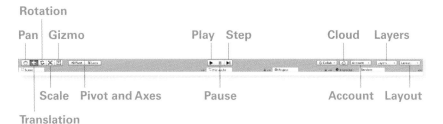

Rotation

Pan | Gizmo   Play   Step   Cloud   Layers

Scale   Pivot and Axes   Pause   Account   Layout

Translation

Figure 2-4: The Toolbar.

Here are the tools you find on the Toolbar:

- **Pan tool:** Grabs onto the screen itself and moves the camera to have a better view of the game objects or world.

- **Translation tool:** Moves your objects along the three axes of 3D (X, Y, and Z).

- **Rotation tool:** Rotates objects around the three axes.

- **Scale tool:** Allows you to adjust the size of your object, making it bigger or smaller along the three axes. The square around the dot is also a scale tool, but it scales from the corners of the object, as opposed to just the center or pivot point.

- **Gizmo tool:** Adjusts where the *pivot point* (the point that your object rotates or scales from) is on the object, as well as what direction of the axes you follow.

- **Play button:** Starts the game, along with any physics or events that start when the game starts. Pressing the Play button again resets the game back to the start.

- **Pause button**: Pauses the game during play.

- **Step button**: Moves the scene frame by frame after playing.

- **Cloud button**: Allows you to access Unity's cloud-based services (see the nearby sidebar).

- **Account drop-down menu**: Allows you to access your Unity account online.

- **Layer drop-down menu**: Allows you to change which layers or objects are visible in the scene.

- **Layout drop-down menu**: Allows you to change Unity's overall layout to better suit your style.

For the purposes of this book, keep the Layout drop-down menu set to 2 by 3.

UNITY'S CLOUD SERVICES

One of Unity's main selling points is its large community and greater opportunities for independent developers to find their way in the field of game development. Unity's cloud services go a long way toward connecting the community together by offering:

- Easy ways to back up your files for a detailed histories of your game's progress

- A place to share your work and get constructive feedback

- A way to connect and share work with other like-minded developers and collaborate on projects that update regularly

- **Inspector window:** The Inspector window allows you to examine and alter the properties of selected objects. These properties change from object to object, so the Inspector window's layout changes the most throughout your work, but knowing how to work in this window is vital to creating games.

- **Hierarchy:** The Hierarchy lists all the game objects in the scene and how they relate to each other. You can use the Scene window to select these objects or select them through the Hierarchy. Think of the Hierarchy as a list of all the things within your project.

- **Console window:** The Console window is at the very bottom of Unity's screen. Its main purpose is to show you messages directly from Unity. Typically, what you'll see here are error messages, often having to do directly with the code of the project. The Console window is most useful when you're coding your game because it helps you narrow down what parts of your game are not functioning and why.

NAVIGATING THE SCENE

Being able to navigate around your scene is important when you're creating your game. You need to be able to move and rotate the scene controls in order to control and create your game. There are three main ways to do that:

- **Panning:** Panning moves up–down or left–right in the scene. If you're using a mouse, you pan by clicking and holding the middle mouse button (the wheel in the middle of the mouse). If you're using a trackpad on a Mac, you pan by clicking and dragging while holding the Alt and Command keys.

- **Rotating:** Rotating moves you around the scene as if you're standing in one place and turning around to see everything around you. You rotate by holding down the Alt key and clicking and dragging on the scene.

- **Zooming:** Zooming moves you closer or farther away from the scene. If you're using a mouse, you zoom by rolling the middle mouse button. If you're using a trackpad on a Mac, you can zoom by using two fingers and sliding them up and down on your trackpad.

CREATING A GAME OBJECT

When you know how to navigate around the scene, you're ready to create and manipulate game objects.

There are two ways to create an object in Unity. You can either select the GameObject menu (near the File and Edit menus) or, under the Hierarchy tab, select the Create drop-down menu. Whichever method you use, choose 3D Object⇨Cube. That's it! You've created a 3D game object!

Before you start playing around with the cube, reset the origin of the cube to be sure it's at the center of the screen. To reset the origin of an object, follow these steps:

1. **Select the object whose origin you want to reset.**

2. **Go to the Inspector window for the object (see Figure 2-5).**

3. **From the Transform menu of the Inspector window, select the gear icon at the upper right.**

4. **Click Reset.**

   The rotation and position are both reset to 0 and the scale is set to 1, centering and resetting the size of the object. This will help you better place and move around your objects in the scene.

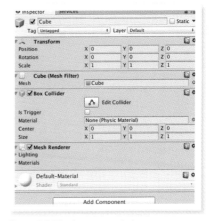

Figure 2-5: The Inspector window.

It also guarantees that all your objects remain at the same axis of rotation and exist in the same scale.

You know how the Toolbar can transform your objects, but there is another more precise way to do this in the Inspector window. The Transformation section of the Inspector window moves, scales, and rotates objects by specific numbers along the set axes:

- **Position** indicates where the box is in relation to the center point of the scene's grid.

- **Rotation** indicates the angle that the box is in relation to each axis.

- **Scale** indicates the scale of the box in relation to its original size.

Play around with these controls to get used them. Then set the Scale of the cube to 4 in the X, Y, and Z (the Position and Rotation should remain 0), as shown in Figure 2-6.

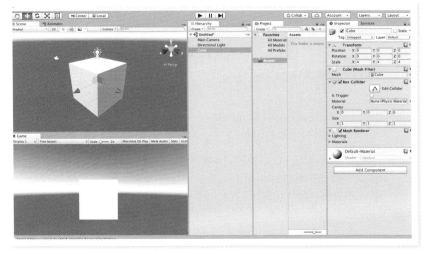

Figure 2-6: Object Reset at 0,0,4.

You've created a cube object, but there are other objects you can create in Unity. Here's a brief overview:

- **3D objects:** These are the normal game objects within 3D games. The 3D objects include the following:

  - Cube

  - Sphere

  - Capsule

  - Cylinder

  - Plane (flat surface)

- Quad (a single face with four sides)

- Rag-doll (a character)

- Terrain

- Tree

- Wind Zone

- 3D Text

- **2D objects:**   There is only one type of 2D object that you can create with this menu: sprites. Sprites are images that you can program to change to show different things for different actions — everything from a character running to a character shooting a gun or talking.

- **Empties:**   Empties are invisible objects that you place in the scene to control or mark something about the scene. They won't show up when you export your game and act only as controls within your game.

- **Lights:**   Lights brighten the scene and can change how the game looks depending on the light setup. Lights are mainly used to brighten the characters and setting and help render a character in 3D.

- **Audio and video:**   The Audio and Video menus help render videos and sounds into your game. These can range from background noise/scenes to music and dialogue.

- **UI:**   *UI* stands for *user interface.* This alters what the player sees onscreen while playing the game. It can range from text informing the player of the controls to images and health bars.

- **Particle systems:**   Particle systems include a variety of different effects that can be seen onscreen, ranging from downpouring water to explosive fire blasts.

- **Cameras:**   Cameras act as the player's eyes into the game. They can be stationary or follow the player around, but their primary purpose is to frame how a game is played. This may not seem important, but the angle at which a game is played can change a lot about the game itself. One example: A first-person shooter framed as a top-down shooter is a vastly different play experience even if the controls are exactly the same.

CREATING AND USING PREFABS

Prefabs are an easy way to create multiple objects that all have the same properties and shapes. Creating non-player characters (NPCs) or in-game objects can be a pain, but with prefabs, you can reuse assets without having to copy and paste them and create multiple individually editable objects.

Prefabs are stored game objects that retain the same properties and can be placed into the game scene at any time. Let's say you have a *collectible* (something that your character needs to pick up). Instead of creating hundreds of the same object over and over again, you can use a prefab to create all of them and adjust the prefab as necessary. Prefabs are easy to use and save a ton of time.

Creating a prefab is easy, but first you want to be sure that you create a folder to store your prefabs in, to keep things organized. Follow these steps:

1. **In the Project window, be sure that nothing else is selected.**

2. **Click Create New Folder.**

   The new folder appears within the Assets folder.

3. **Name the new folder Prefabs.**

4. **Select the object that you want to turn into a prefab — in this case, the 4x4x4 cube.**

5. **Drag the object from the Hierarchy into the Prefabs folder in the Project window.**

   A prefab of the object is created, as shown in Figure 2-7.

After creating a prefab, you can select the prefab in the Project window to alter and add new components to all the prefabs in the scene. For example, you can change the size of the object, change its color, or give it gravity.

Try adding the component Rigidbody to the prefab you have in the Project window and see what happens:

1. **Click Add Component.**

2. **Select Physics.**

3. **Select Rigidbody.**

4. **Press Play on the Toolbar.**

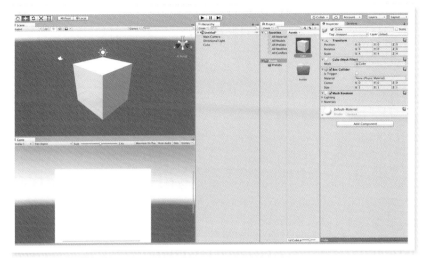

Figure 2-7: Prefabs.

The cube(s) fall through the sky. This is because you just added gravity to them. I touch on the Rigidbody component more in Chapter 4, but for now, follow these steps:

1. **Click the Play button again to reset the game.**

2. **Choose 3D Object ⇨ Plane.**

   This will create a plane in the Scene window.

3. **Reset the plane's origin in the Inspector window, as you did with the cube earlier (using the gear in the upper right of the Inspector window).**

4. **Use the Translation tools to move the cube along the y-axis so that it's under the box.**

Creating Level 1

In this chapter, you learn some of the core concepts behind your first level and how to design a good introductory level to your game. Beyond that, this chapter will also teach you some basics about level design, which you'll be able to use going forward to design your own unique levels for your future games.

In order to create clear and interesting levels, you have to start off by thinking of them not in their final polished forms but from their most basic beginnings. A game with pretty images and dull mechanics is just a boring game, but designers have been drawing people into games for years, starting back when they were only a few pixels on a screen.

This chapter shows you how to set aside your theme while you design so that you can create the most compelling gameplay possible from the beginning.

UNDERSTANDING THE IMPORTANCE OF LEVEL 1

In books or movies, the first ten pages or minutes matter. These are your hooks, what introduces the audience to the world and grabs their attention. It's the title crawl that leads into an epic chase in *Star Wars,* or the curious day in the life of Vernon Dursley that ends with a lightning-scarred boy on his doorstep in *Harry Potter.* These introductions act as gateways to much larger and more complex stories, getting your attention so that when the actual plot begins, you're already invested. In a computer game, this hook is Level 1.

In a game, the first major thing you have to sell to a player is the *core mechanics* (the main controls or features of your game). In a platformer, these are the controls that let you run and jump; in a choice-based story game, these mechanics may be the dialogue trees. The first level can be tough to design, because you have to introduce your player to the game without the game harshly punishing them for making a mistake. At the same time, you don't want the first level to be boring. You have to introduce concepts slowly but emphasize the need for urgency to learn those mechanics.

Although not as important as mechanics, the first level also has to introduce players to the world that they'll be playing in. Interesting worlds and stories are accomplished partly through dialogue and *cutscenes* (short scenes that the player watches but has little to no control in). They can also be achieved through visuals and design choices.

There are some great examples of first levels (or opening minutes) in gaming history — Super Mario Bros. (see Figure 3-1), Super Meat Boy (see Figure 3-2), and Mass Effect 2 (see Figure 3-3), to name just a few. None of these games' first levels or opening minutes feel superfluous. They present only the necessary information for players to better understand the game. Even Mass Effect 2, which presents a gorgeous display of a planet in the background, doesn't feel excessive because the level is supposed to inspire a sense of awe and wonder.

REMEMBER

Creating a first level that has too much going on can be just as dangerous as creating a first level that's boring. Before designing the level, figure out what your player needs to know and build from there. You can fill later levels with insane obstacles and crazy set pieces, but there has to be a natural sense of progression within the game, especially when it comes to the mechanics of the game.

Figure 3-1: Mario's World 1-1.

Figure 3-2: Super Meat Boy World 1-1.

Figure 3-3: Mass Effect 2 opening.

DESIGNING YOUR FIRST LEVEL

Designing your first level is similar to trying to solve your first algebraic equation or make your first layup: You won't get it perfect the first time. In fact, it's impossible to design a perfect level on your first attempt, so don't stress about it!

Design is all about refining and asking questions. Keep practicing and seeing what works and what doesn't, until your Level 1 is just right.

THINKING ABOUT MECHANICS AND THEME

Before starting your game, make sure you know what core mechanics you want in the game. This information will be helpful when you start designing your level. Ask yourself what the mechanics of your game are, and understand how those mechanics relate to the theme of your game.

Knowing not only your mechanics but the story they relate to will help you figure out the best way to introduce the different controls of the game and in what order. Do your mechanics and theme fit with a traditional tutorial? Or does the game lend itself to a subtler approach?

When you start designing Level 1, think about the best way to introduce your player to the game. Should you start with a more action-packed scene to put the player directly into the world? Or should your game start off with a calmer approach?

The game you'll be building in this book is a 3D platformer that takes place in a cartoony world. Because of this, you'll be following the Super Mario Bros. format by slowly introducing concepts through the level and gradually increasing the difficulty as the level progresses.

REMEMBER

The major point of the rough draft is to get an idea of the basic aspects of your level. What are the enemies of the level going to be? How are you going to introduce players to the concepts of the level? What is the level going to look like?

DRAWING THE ROUGH DRAFTS

Before worrying about specific measurements or the scale of your level, you need to get an idea of what your level will look like. For this, I suggest you use a blank piece of paper or a white board so that you can erase and rework your ideas as you get them. Think of this process as being similar to an outline for an essay. It allows you to get all your ideas out in an unpolished fashion. Then you can refine, add, and cut as you please.

This is an outline, so don't worry about the details. Just focus on the overall look of the level.

In the example in Figure 3-4, you can see notes on what are important in the level. I've included the enemies, inclines, and drops as important parts of the games design. You also see some moving platforms, as well as some spikes toward the end of the level. This isn't a perfect representation of what the final level will look like, but it gives a solid idea of what needs to be translated into the more in-depth design of the level.

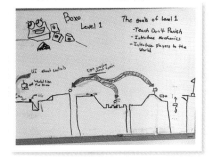

Figure 3-4: Boxo Level 1 draft.

Use this time to consider how players are introduced to new mechanics or aspects of your game. Level 1 shouldn't just start with steep drops or punishing game moments. It should be a learning experience that builds on what happened earlier. Later levels can up the difficulty, but without proper early levels teaching the player about the mechanics, any later difficulty spikes will feel unearned or even harsh to new players.

REMEMBER

When you design your first draft, leave room for interpretation and don't be discouraged by imperfect ideas. This step is just to help you get your ideas out on paper.

You never want your player to feel cheated by your game, so give players time to learn the tricks of the game before pushing them into the deep end. If you introduce difficulty correctly, the payoff to completing the level will outweigh the frustration of failure.

GRAPHING YOUR FIRST LEVEL TO SCALE

After you build the outline of your level, it's time to figure out the scale of the level. The best way to do this is to use a grid or some graph paper to draw out a more finalized design of your level. Figure out a ratio of box-to-unit measurement in Unity before you begin drawing. But once you figure out that ratio, you should draw out a more fully realized level based on your designs from earlier.

Figure 3-5 uses a one-to-one scale with each box on the grid representing one unit of measurement within Unity. In Chapters 9 and 12, I cover how Unity's scale relates to other programs such as Blender, but for now you just need to recognize how objects relate to each other in Unity's scale. From a cursory glance at Figure 3-5, you'll notice that Boxy (the player character) is four units large in Unity. Keep the scale of the character in mind while designing the rest of the level. Everything in the level is based on the scale of Boxy and is designed around the scale of the character.

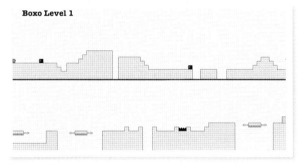

Figure 3-5: Boxo Level 1.

Why does scale matter in game design?

- **It helps you determine the difficulty and understand the necessary movement requirements of your characters.**   If you determine that a character's max jump distance is five units, you won't create distances that are impossible for the character to overcome.

- **It helps you keep track of how objects relate to each other.**   If a wall and spike path are properly scaled, you're more easily able to build an interesting level.

Using graph paper, you'll be better able to translate that scale into your game and will more effectively be able to build your game. Keeping scale will prevent you from building objects or scenery that doesn't fit to scale with the rest of the environment. It would be very jarring for your character to climb a staircase only to come to a wall that is impossible to get past because the scale is off and doesn't match how high your character can jump. *Remember:* Organization saves lives — and that goes for your scale as well.

CREATING THE GRAY-BOX LEVEL

A *gray-box level* is the bare minimum design of your game that you need to make the game playable. Think of it as a practice run to make sure that your game works on a mechanical level without theme getting in the way.

Gray-box levels are similar to storyboards in film, which are a way to visually express a film before any filming is actually done. In film, story-boards are used to check whether a story is understandable when it's presented. Although some of the more glaring issues can be caught through script readings and editing, storyboards gives filmmakers a chance to see which parts of the film work and which parts don't work when they're presented as a whole, sequentially. Sometimes storyboards might help the filmmaker to see that she needs to move a scene or two around or remove scenes or storylines entirely to make the film flow better.

Level design is similar. Although you can see some glaring issues in the early level drafts and drawings, you can't catch all of the problems until players have a chance to play it for themselves. By creating a gray-box level, you're able to program and fix your game before you put too much effort into making the game look good.

You want to find any problems with the game before you spend hours building a detailed environment around those bugs. Finding bugs early is key to creating a good game! Think of your gray-box level as your test run. You're making sure the mechanics of the game work and are fun before you spend hours on a project only to discover that the game is broken on a fundamental level. The earlier you discover the failings of your game, the less heart-breaking it will be for you.

CREATING YOUR PREFABS

The first thing you want to do when you open Unity to build your level is to create all the prefabs that will be used throughout your game. Keep in mind that for the game that you'll be designing throughout this book, the direction the character travels is along the *z*-axis (left to right).

Look through your latest design of your level and make note of all the objects or charac-ters that are used multiple times throughout

REMEMBER

Prefabs are objects within the game that you can create multiples of and have the ability to alter all at once without needing to change each one individually. Prefabs are especially useful for objects that you'll be using a lot of throughout the levels, such as stairs and walls. (See Chapter 2 for more on prefabs.)

the level. I cover how to construct animated characters or objects in Chapters 9 and 10, but for now, simple stand-ins for these animations will do just fine. In Figure 3-2, there are several different prefabs that you can create, including some stairs, walls, and a stand-in for the moving platforms that you'll include later.

Let's start with the stairs. To do that, you'll work with a cube. Follow these steps:

1. **Create a cube, and reset the cube's position and rotation by clicking the gear in the upper right of the Inspector.**

2. **Set the scale of the cube to (X=8, Y=2, Z=6).**
   This creates the bottom step of the three-step staircase. If you want a longer staircase, increase the Z scale.

3. **Set the name of the cube to "Stairs."**

4. **Create a new cube, and reset its position and rotation.**

5. **Set the scale to (X=8, Y=2, Z=4).**
   This stair step has to be a little shorter than the previous one because there has to be a gradual progression.

6. **Change the position of this cube to (X=0, Y=2, Z=1).**

The object is moved from its center or pivot point. In the objects you'll be creating in this game, both are at the center of the object. Whenever you move the object, keep in mind that it moves from its center. If an object has a total size of 1, that means that if you want to move it so one end is touching a line, you have to add 0.5 to whatever the location of the line is.

7. **Rename the cube to "Step 2" using the Inspector.**

8. **Create a third cube, and reset its position and rotation.**

9. Set the scale to (X=8, Y=2, Z=2).

10. Change the position of this cube to (X=0, Y=4, Z=2).

11. Rename the cube to "Step 3" using the Inspector.
    See Figure 3-6 for an example of what you should have.

Figure 3-6: Stairs.

12. Using the hierarchy menu drag Step 3 into Step 2 to create a Parent. Then drag Step 2 into Stairs to parent both Step 2 and Step 3 to Stairs.
    Parents control children (at least in games!). When an object is parented to something, it means that the object is affected by the rotation, translation, and scale of that object. When the parent is changed, so is the child, but the child's personal scale, rotation, and translation remains unaffected, which will be important when we bring animated objects into the game in Chapter 12.

REMEMBER

Have you saved? Now would be a great time to do so! Press Ctrl+S (Windows) or Command+S (Mac) to save your game.

13. Drag Stairs from the Hierarchy menu into the previously created Prefabs folder (see Chapter 2) to create a Stairs prefab that will actually change not only Stairs but also the objects parented to the stairs.

Saving is wonderful, but there are two types of saves in Unity: Save Scene and Save Project. Save Scene will save whatever scene you're currently working on in your game, so any changes you make within your scene will be saved. Save Project will *only* save things that affect the wider project, such as interactions between scenes. Saving Project will *not* save your scene, and you'll lose any changes you make. Be sure to choose the right version of save; otherwise, you could lose a lot of vital work. The keyboard shortcut saves the scene, not the project.

After you create your stairs prefab, you'll notice when you select it that in the Inspector there is now a Prefab section near the top. Next to "Prefab," there are three buttons:

- **Select**: Selects the Prefab in the Project window

- **Revert**: Undoes any changes you made to your prefab back to the standard prefab settings

- **Apply**: Changes *all* of the objects that go off that prefab to match the one you've selected

To test this out, follow these steps:

1. **Drag out a second and third staircase onto the Scene window.**

2. **Create a new material using the Create drop-down in the Project window and choose Material.**

3. **Change the color of the material.**

4. **Drag that new material to one of the staircases.**

5. **Select the staircase and click Apply.**

   All your objects that go off of that prefab will now change to match this color.

Now delete the staircase. You don't need to worry about having to do it again. After you create a prefab of the object, Unity will automatically have a copy of the prefab to refer to. So now whenever you need stairs, you'll be able to simply drag and drop the stairs into the scene.

The next prefabs that you should create are

- **A wall**: The walls should be tall enough that your character has to jump over them and wide enough to prevent players from simply walking around them. For the purposes of the game in this book the X-scale should be 30, because that will be how wide our level will be. The wall measurements should be (X=30, Y=2, Z=2).

- **A stand-in for the moving platforms**: As a stand-in for moving platforms, you'll create planks that will go across the long gaps between some sections of the level. These planks should be much thinner than the walls or stairs and should be easy to climb on. They also need to be long across the Z-axis to reach across. Using Figure 3-2, you can determine that one of these planks need to be at least 31 long. The plank measurements should be (X=4, Y=0.5, Z=31).

- **Stand-ins for the enemy characters and spikes:** The enemy character stand-ins can just be still moving cubes for now, located at the
center point of where the enemy characters will be moving in. You'll
be animating their movement in Blender, so you only need a still
stand-in for the purposes of building the level and to test the death
mechanics with. The enemy stand-in measurements should be (X=2,
Y=2, Z=2).

    The spikes will also be made in Blender, so you'll be using a similar
    stand-in for those. You don't need any fancy characters or objects
    because the purpose of the gray-box level is to test the game mechan-
    ically. Squares, spheres, capsules, and cylinders work just as well
    for designing the game as any character would. The spike stand-in
    measurements should be (X=1, Y=1, Z=1).

Be sure you drag all of these different objects from
the hierarchy window into the Prefabs folder so that
you can access them later.

REMEMBER

Save your work.

BUILDING YOUR LEVEL

Now that you have all your prefabs made, it's time to actually start building the first level of your game. When you begin your game, you need
to start by building the base of all your platforms before adding any of
the prefabs. Graph paper will help you figure out how long each section
should be.

As an example, the first platform in Figure 3-2 has the measurements
(X=30, Y=4, Z=56). The first platform has an indent in it, so only measure
up to that indent to find the starting height you need to plug in for your
platform. Create a cube and use the values above to scale it to its proper
size. Then change the Y-position to 2 so that the bottom of the cube is on
the platform, and change the X-position of the cube to 28 so that the back
of the cube is at the 0 location.

After you place the base of your first platform and reset the location and
rotation back to 0, it's time to build up on top of that platform:

1. **Create two more cubes, and reset their rotation scale and position**.

2. **Change the Y-scale of both to 6 and the X-scale to 30.**

3. **Change the Y position of both to 7.**

    Normally this would be 5 but because we changed the bottom
    platform so that the bottom of the platform is on the grid, objects
    on top of the platform have to be twice as high.

4. **Change one cube's Z-scale to 24 and its Z-position to 12 so that it is placed at the top and front of the platform.**

5. **Change the other cube's Z-scale to 23 and its Z-position to 44.5 (see Figure 3-7 as an example).**

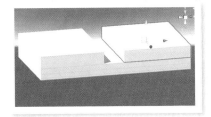

Figure 3-7: Starting platform.

To finish up this platform, there is still one cube that has to be placed at the top of the platform.

6. **After you create this cube, reset its rotation, scale, and location.**

TIP

You should always do this out of habit. Resetting your location, rotation, or scale right at the start will prevent you from ever accidentally parenting or scaling something the wrong way. If an object is placed and not reset, when it's parented it isn't parented from 0,0,0, which can cause issues later on in the actual gameplay performance by causing certain objects to end up in the wrong spot. Resetting from the get-go prevents this.

7. **Change the scale of the cube to (X=30 Y=6 Z=11).**

8. **Change the location of the cube to (X=0 Y=13 Z=50.5).**

After finishing up building the first platform, start measuring and creating the second platform, which is three units away. Figure 3-8 gives a breakdown of all the measurements to create the level. Reference it when creating the rest of the level.

Whenever you're trying to place an object, add half their size to the point you're trying to move them to. For example, if on the grid the Z-position (the pink line going vertically) reads Z = 114, you would have to add half the size of the object to properly place it on the z-axis. So the Z-position of that platform would be 114 + (54 ÷ 2) = 114 + 27 = 141.

The horizontal lines represent the Y-positions, and the same math has to be used to place the cubes and platforms along that axis.

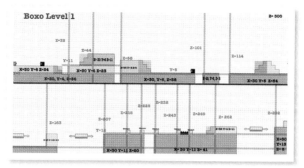

Figure 3-8: Level 1 with number breakdown.

PLACING YOUR PREFABS

After you finish building the base platforms of the level, it's now time to begin placing your prefabs throughout the level. Let's start with the stairs. Open your Prefabs folder and drag a staircase out.

At this point, you can do a very similar thing to what you did earlier, but there's actually another way to place objects. By pressing V on your keyboard, you activate Vertex Snapping, which will allow you to grab a *vertex* (corner) of a GameObject and *snap* (place directly) to another object's vertex. This can save you a lot of time and headache when building out a level — especially when you need to place a GameObject on a level that doesn't have as precise measurements as we've been working with.

The problem with Vertex Snapping is that it only really works within Unity's orthographic views.

Orthographic views flatten out a 3D object so that you can view it in 2D. This helps when you want to place objects in certain spots because you naturally want to convert images into 2D shapes. By working in Orthographic mode and alternating between the top, right, and front views, you're able to get a more realized and precisely placed design for your level. You can switch between Orthographic and Perspective modes by clicking the tiny cube in the upper-right corner of the scene window. If you click the X, Z, or Y cones around it, they'll bring you to the Front (Z), Right (X), or Top(Y) views.

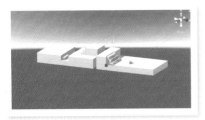

Figure 3-9: Level 1 with stairs.

Another shortcut that can help you place objects on top of each other without having to do as much math is the Surface Snapping tool. Press Shift+Ctrl (Windows) or Shift+Command (Mac), and you'll be able to move objects so that they'll snap to the surfaces of other objects, making it far easier to place things like stairs, monsters, or planks.

First, begin by using Surface Snapping to place the stairs on the level. See Figure 3-9 for an example of how it should look.

You'll immediately notice that the stairs are too big for the middle section in between the two upper platforms. Luckily, one of the great things about prefabs is that you can alter one without altering all the others in the scene. Simply delete the top step of the stairs and rotate and place it into the proper spot. As long as you don't hit the Apply button in the Inspector, this change won't affect the other prefabs in the scene.

REMEMBER

Save your work.

After you finish placing all the stairs in the scene, you'll begin placing the plank stand-ins for the moving platforms. Because these will be acting as stand-ins until you can create moving objects in Blender, you want them to still give a similar sense of challenge that the moving platforms will when they're added in. The best way to do this is to place the planks across the gaps but at an angle, as in Figure 3-10. When placing the planks, you'll notice that they may not be big enough or may be too big for the gap you created. As with the stairs, you can alter the shape and size of these planks to better fit your needs without altering the rest of the prefabs in the sequence.

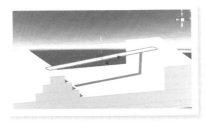

Figure 3-10: The planks being placed across the gaps.

At this stage, you want your game to be the bare bones of what your eventual game will end up being. Do your best to capture the overall feeling you're aiming to go for in this game, even at this stage. Creating the tension of walking across a narrow plank can give the same fear of falling as jumping from a moving platform. Always think about how your player may react to a situation. You can even make it so that the player actually has to jump between two different planks to get to the other side just to add a sense of tension because of height.

Go further into your level and customize it more to fit what you want it to be. Add more planks or obstacles that the player has to overcome. Add more placeholders for when you make enemies to place in Chapters 9 through 12.

Game design is about making a game that you would want to play. When you're designing a level, ask yourself what would intrigue you and add it in.

After you finish your level, make sure that you aren't missing anything or that there aren't gaps too big for the player. Make sure the game has a logical sense of progression that will reward the player and not punish them. Adjust where necessary. See Figure 3-11 as an example.

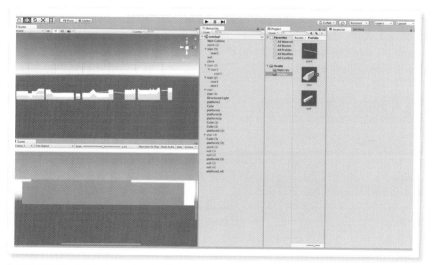

Figure 3-11: The finished gray-box level.

GIVING YOUR LEVEL OBJECTIVE AND DIRECTION

Objectives are the lifeblood of a game. Without a clear objective, players don't know why they're playing. When you're designing your first level, you have to decide what the goal of the player is. Is it to save the prince from the castle, to survive until 6 a.m., or to escape a zombie-infested city?

Building an objective — especially an objective in a level — is a huge part of level design. Objectives have to stand out to the player and draw the player's attention. Often in videogames, a lot is going at once. Even in a game like Super Mario Bros., there are a ton of creatures waddling around that try to demand the player's attention. So how, as a game designer, do you build an objective that can stand out?

In the case of Super Mario Bros., the objective was built into the mystery of going further to discover more. It may seem strange, but part of the thrill of playing Super Mario Bros. was that you never knew what was going to come next! You had to be prepared for all sorts of monsters, as indicated early on in the game. The main objective was to rescue the princess, but the minor objective of each level was to get to the flag at the end.

Other games use other techniques to indicate direction. Some use coins or pickup items to give the player something to follow. Other games give players direction by putting them into a dark room and having only one door lit up at the end. Sometimes objectives fuel direction; other times direction fuels objectives. As players, we hunt for answers to these questions. We want to know what the purpose of the game is. As a designer, your job is to clearly indicate where the player should be going and reward the player for going there, either by giving the player more coins or by advancing the plot.

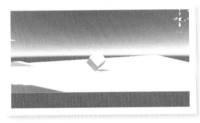

When you finish designing your level, you have to give the player a reason to go forward. For the purposes of your platformer, this reasoning will be items that the player can collect while going through the game. The following steps will take you through how to create a pickup item (see Figure 3-12):

Figure 3-12: Pickup item.

1. **Create a cube, sphere, or cylinder that will act as the pickup item in the game.**

2. **Name the GameObject "Pickup."**

3. **Create a prefab for this object.**

4. **Begin placing the object copies throughout your level.**

   You can even place some in the air where the character will be encouraged to jump.

   By setting the object around the level leading from the beginning to the end, you give your player a path for them to follow.

The pickup item doesn't really stand out from the background. So, how do you make the pickup item stand out from the rest of the scene? There are multiple ways to do this:

- You can have the object be moving slightly.

- You can put a light on the object so it glows when you look toward it.

- You can make the object an unusual shape or size compared to the things around it.

- You change the object's color or hue so it stands out from the background.

For this chapter, you'll be following the last example. You already placed all the objectives around the map, but the use of prefabs prevents this from being a far more tedious task than it needs to be. Simply create a new material and apply it to an object (see Figure 3-13).

Figure 3-13: A standout objective.

After you've applied the material to the object, go to the Inspector and click Apply. Your color will be applied to all the objective prefabs. Now you have a level with objectives that not only stand out but lead players in the direction you want them to go!

REMEMBER

Save your work!

04

Camera, Character, and Controls

In this chapter, you'll be learning the fundamental basis behind game development: coding. This chapter explains how you can make your game interactive so that people will be able to *play* your game. I'll show you a simple movement code that you can use as a jumping-off point for coding in the future. I'll also explain the different aspects of the code and the core thoughts behind every piece of code.

Here, you'll also learn how to program your character so that she'll pick up the pickup items you created in Chapter 3, which involves creating and applying object tags. You'll learn about how to write a simple code that will allow your camera to follow your character through the level. These codes will act as an introduction to some more complex codes that I'll cover in Chapter 5. What you'll learn in this chapter will be expanded upon in the next chapter.

THE THREE CS OF GAME DEVELOPMENT

When you make a game, keep in mind the three Cs of game development: camera, character, and control. These three Cs act as the player's main introduction into the world that you hope to create. They're the only aspects of your game that your player will always be dealing with. When you understand the role of each of these three Cs in your game, you'll better understand not only your game, but all games that you create or play.

CAMERA

The camera is the player's window into your game. It's what the player sees and responds to. Camera placement in a game is vital because the player's basic understanding of your game world will come through the camera.

In film, the camera shows only what the cinematographer and director want the audience to see. Changing the location of the camera can change the entire feeling of the scene or, in some cases, break the scene entirely.

Your game camera should be treated in much the same way as a film camera. The problem is that, in games, you can't always control where the player (or camera) goes. When you create your camera, you have to decide how much control you want your player to have over the camera and whether you'll limit that control in any way. A camera that is locked behind the player character will reveal different information than one that is located above or to the side of the player character. Cameras that players have complete control over or that players can rotate reveal to the player informa- tion from all over the world — but they may also reveal aspects of the game that you wouldn't otherwise want players to see.

CHARACTER

The character is who the player is playing as in the game. This can be deceptive because the theme of the character doesn't matter at this point in game development. Whether the char-

REMEMBER

Cameras are all about revealing information to the player. When you design your game camera, ask yourself what in your game is the most import- ant for your player to know and what you want to keep hidden.

acter is a super-detailed soldier or a box is irrelevant when you're coding your game. What you need to think about when you think of character is what exactly your character does within the game. Ask yourself the following questions:

- Does the character jump? If so, how high?

- Does the character have four-directional movement (forward, backward, left, right) or does the character only move forward and backward?

- Does my character have any weapons or tools? If so, what are they?

How your character moves not only changes what your game is but how you'll go about coding your game. A first-person shooter has an entirely different code than a platformer. Even different types of platformers can have a variety of different codes simply because of the types of controls you want the character to have.

CONTROL

Control is how your player interacts with the game. The thing that separates games from every other type of entertainment medium is their unique ability to engage with an audience. Players don't just read or watch the events play out as they do with books, movies, or TV shows. They play an active role in the experience and are invested in the charac- ters because they *are* the characters.

Controls make or break a game. A game with a poor control setup will never engage players on the same level as one with good controls, no matter how good the graphics or story is. You play games because they make you feel in control, so when you design your game, you have to think about how controls interact with the player and how you can make the game accessible for the greatest number of people.

For example, when you think about movement in a computer game, what buttons do you think of? Probably the W, A, S, and D keys. But why? Why don't gamed designers use the 6, Caps Lock, Enter, and Spacebar keys instead? After all, those keys also relate to the different directions. The reason designers typically use W, A, S, and D is because they don't want the player to have to put a lot of effort into playing the game for each desired effect. If you have to move your hand too much, or stop and think about the controls, that can break your immersion in the game, which kills it. You want the time it takes for a player to think of something and the time it takes for her to enact it to be minimal so that players never break their immersion within the game.

REMEMBER

Too many controls, confusing controls, or just awkwardly spaced controls can prevent players from ever becoming too invested in a game. Think about games that have felt like they just flow naturally when you play them. This is likely because the controls have been designed so that players have to put in minimal thought to accomplish what they want to do. This doesn't mean that there can't be complex combinations that come from mastering these controls (think of how fighting games combos work). But these complexities should come naturally and flow with the game. When you're designing controls, think about how you want your game to flow.

CREATING A CHARACTER STAND-IN

In Chapter 3, you created a completed gray-box level to act as the skeleton for your game. This gray-box level (shown in Figure 4-1) allowed you to test out the controls and make sure the game as a whole was fun before you added the *skin* (the exterior look for the game — character designs, settings, and so on). A gray-box level is an unpolished base for your game that you can use to test your game before you spend hours creating characters and other assets that will make up your overall game.

Figure 4-1: The completed gray-box level.

Similarly, character stand-ins are a way for you to program and test your character, controls, and camera without needing to invest time in creating a detailed character first. Stand-ins help you focus on your character's fundamental controls and movements without being tempted to focus too heavily on the theme of your character. You're forced to think primarily about the player's enjoyment of the game rather than the game itself.

As with the gray-box level, your character stand-in doesn't need to be super complex to get the point across. The one thing a stand-in character should do is stand apart from the background. To create your stand-in character, follow these steps:

REMEMBER

Always keep your player in mind when you're designing your game. You can think you have the greatest game in the world, but if no one wants to play it, it doesn't accomplish the one goal all games have: to be played!

1. **Go to GameObject and create a Cube.**

2. **Drag the cube to the start of the level using the translation tools.**

   It doesn't need to be placed directly on the top of the level, but it should be above it at the very least.

3. Go to your Assets folder in your project window, and create a new folder called Materials.

4. Move any existing materials into this folder.

5. Create a new material, and apply it to the cube.

6. Change the color of the material so that the player distinctly stands out from the background.

See Figure 4-2 for what the character should look like.

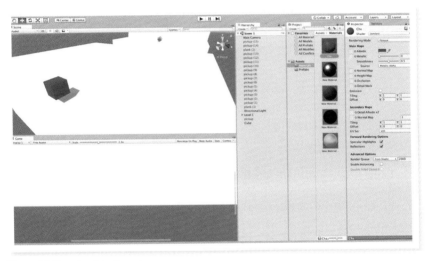

Figure 4-2: Your stand-in character.

Save your scene and project.

THINKING ABOUT CODE

What is coding? When you think about coding, you probably think about movie hackers shifting through walls of ones and zeroes to crack the code into the vault or something. You think of it as something that requires a bunch of math and computing to figure out.

Coding does rely on math, but its more akin to learning a new language than doing math. Coding is just telling the computer or game what you want it to do in a language that it can understand. The problem is that computers are stupid, so when you code, you have to code *everything*.

For example, let's say you have a robot and you want to program it to make a peanut butter and jelly sandwich. In order to do this, you have to program each step involved in creating this sandwich. Try writing out all the steps that are needed to create a peanut butter jelly sandwich and then come back to this book. I'll wait!

It's very likely that the list you came up with isn't as detailed as it needs to be. In order to program a robot to make a peanut butter and jelly sandwich you have to have these steps:

1. Turn to point toward cabinet.

2. Move toward cabinet.

3. Open hand.

4. Rotate arm up to handle.

5. Close hand around handle.

6. Open cabinet.

7. Release handle.

8. Move hand to peanut butter.

9. Grab peanut butter.

10. Take peanut butter out of cabinet.

11. Put peanut butter on counter.

12. Move hand to jelly.

And these are just the steps for taking out the peanut butter and jelly! In the real code, you would have to program what the total distance of a step is for the robot and how many steps it requires to go to the cabinet. You would also have to program it to know what jelly and peanut butter are, as well as bread slices, a plate, and a knife.

Coding is all about laying out clear directions for the computer to follow. In games, your code not only has to act on its own, but also has to react to what the player does within the game.

REMEMBER

Computers are stupid.

ADDING RIGIDBODY COMPONENT AND UNDERSTANDING BOX COLLIDERS

Before you begin to code your character, Unity offers a way for you to easily apply physics and other forces to your object. You don't have to worry about coding gravity and other forces because it's all included in the Rigidbody component. The Rigidbody component makes it so that outside forces and objects can actually have an effect on the object within the game.

For example, let's say you make a cube in an empty scene. When you click Play, without a Rigidbody constraint, the cube will remain in the air because the cube is unaffected by any outside forces and will stay still. If you were to add a Rigidbody component to the cube and then click Play, the cube would fall forever because there is nothing keeping it up. Now that gravity can be applied to it, it will fall infinitely. If you were to add a separate object or plane below the cube, the cube would land on that object or plane. This is because of another component that is already added to all the 3D objects: a collider.

A *collider* is an invisible outline that wraps around the 3D game objects that signals when one object "collides" with another object. The colliders of different objects interact with each other and signal when two objects touch. You can access the collider by selecting your object and going to the Inspector window. You can adjust the size of a collider to be larger or smaller than the object.

Colliders indicate when two objects interact. Having a smaller or larger collider can change how far away a character has to be to interact with another object, and even what parts of the character will interact with another object. If your character is human and has a box collider around them, then a hit can register even if the character's body isn't touching anything.

You can also adjust the center point of the collider, which will move it around your object. Most objects have a collider naturally, but if they don't, you can always add a collider.

To add a collider, follow these steps:

1. **In the Inspector window, at the bottom you'll see an Add Component button.**

2. **Click Add Component and then select Physics.**

3. **From the Physics menu, select your desired collider (see Figure 4-3).**

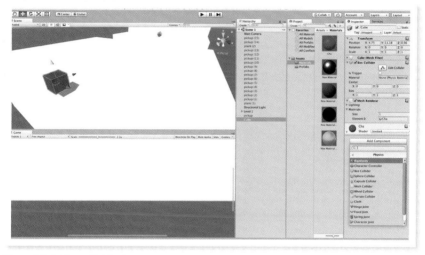

Figure 4-3: Adding a Rigidbody component.

Different colliders have different shapes. A mesh collider is the most versatile. It's able to wrap around different types of meshes. You can also use the Add Component button to add multiple colliders to an bject.

Adding a Rigidbody component to the player character will make it so that you can give your character the ability to jump and fall on top of the basic forward and sideway movements. To add a Rigidbody to your character, first make sure that you have the right object selected in your Scene window. Then follow steps 1 through 2 from earlier. When you get to Step 3, instead of selecting the collider, select Rigidbody.

To test the Rigidbody on your object, simply click the Play button on the top of the screen. The object should fall and land on the level that you created. Now that your object is affected by gravity, it's time to program it so that you can make it move and jump around using the keyboard.

REMEMBER

Save your scene and project.

CODING YOUR PLAYER

When you create code in Unity, you actually create the code separately from the object and later attach it to the object, as opposed to coding to the object directly. The benefit to this approach is that you're easily able to transfer the code you create to other objects as you create them, making the transfer from a gray-box level and stand-in character incredibly simple. But this means that you need to create the code separate and have it stored someplace else.

The first step is to create a new folder in your assets folder in the Project window and name the folder Code. This will be where you store all the codes you'll be making in this game. It's a good habit to get into — proper organization can save you hours of superfluous work.

After you create a folder to store all your code in, you have to create the file that you'll use to write your code in:

1. **Make sure that the Code folder is selected.**

2. **Click Create.**

3. **Choose Create ⇨ C# Script.**

4. **Name the script Char (short for character), as shown in Figure 4-4.**

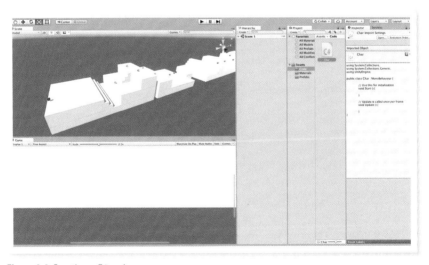

Figure 4-4: Creating a C# code.

This will create a C# code that you'll be able to go into and change to include the code for your character. There are many different languages in coding. For the purposes of this project, you'll be using C# (pronounced "C Sharp"). C# is a powerful programing language used in Unity and a variety of other programs. It's type-safe and focuses on object-oriented goals within the code (for example, "Do this thing and this happens").

Selecting the C# code and double-clicking it will open up Unity's included code-writing software, MonoDevelop (shown in Figure 4-5). When MonoDevelop opens, you'll see what looks at first like a word-processing program but with the lines clearly numbered. This is the basic code-writing software that you'll use when making your Unity games.

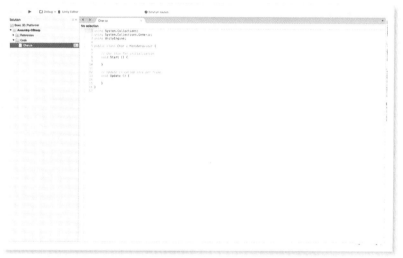

Figure 4-5: MonoDevelop.

When you open this code, you'll notice that part of the code is already written out for you. Unity automatically writes some of the basic parts of the code for you when it creates a new script. To better understand coding, let's breakdown what every part of this code is doing for the game as a whole, using Figure 4-5 as a reference point.

The first three lines of this code determine the systems and engines that the code will be accessing in the code as reference. You'll notice that the first two are System.Collections and System.Collections.Generic.

These are the two namespaces that give access to a variety of codes and classes that will be used in C#. These are aspects of the code that make up the bulk of how your codes will be working. On line 3, the code is accessing the Unity engine, which indicates that it will be controlling some basic aspects through the Untiy engine. Later in this chapter, you'll be adding a new engine for the code to access and alter, but for now, just leave it alone.

Note how there are spaces between the different sections of Unity's code. These spaces act simply as ways to break up large blocks of code and make the code more accessible and readable. There is no reason within the code to break apart the lines, but by doing so you'll create a code that is easier to understand and work in. When you code, be sure to create breaks within the code to give yourself more space to work in.

In C#, classes act as templates that classify game objects within the code. A `void` acts as an indicator that the following method will not accept any parameters and will not return any value back. A `void Start` indicates a method that will begin at the start of the game (when you first press the Play button). A `void Update` updates every frame of the game.

Whenever you see `//` in code, it indicates a dead line of code. When `//` is added in a line, everything following that grays out to indicate that it's no longer active. Often programmers use `//` as a way to make notes within the code that can help them better understand what's going on in the code. Other punctuation in coding has purposes of their own. These are the most common within coding:

- { } indicates the start and end points of a particular string. A string is a particular part of the code. You can have multiple strings within each other in a code.

- ( ) acts as further qualification for a method to begin. You'll use these in `if` statements to set up why a certain code will begin when it begins.

- ; indicates the end of a particular line of code. Think of semicolons as the period in a sentence of the code while the { } indicates the total paragraph or essay.

Now that you've examined some of the starting code, it's time to add your code into the mix. You'll start with a simple movement code that indicates how fast the character will move, what direction it will move in, and when it will move.

In Figure 4-6, you'll notice that a `public float` was added underneath the class. Floats act as a reference point that later parts of the code can use. In this case, you can see that the code reads `public float Speed = 5f;`. In this case, `public float` indicates the type of code that you're creating, `Speed` is the name of the float you're creating, = indicates that the following number directly relates and changes the `Speed`, and `5f` stands for 5 float integers. So whatever is affected by `Speed` will change by 5 of a particular integer.

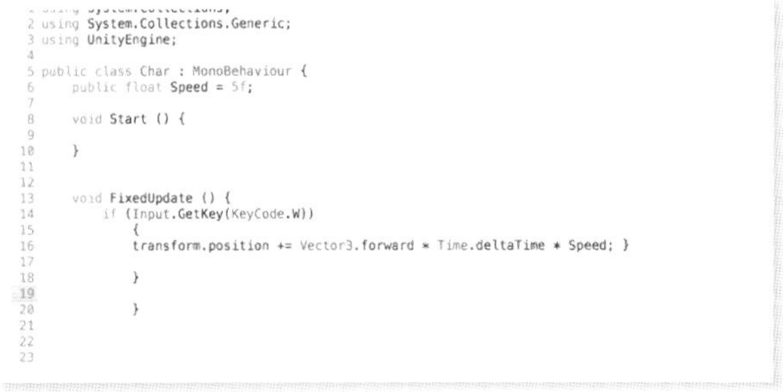

```
2 using System.Collections.Generic;
3 using UnityEngine;
4
5 public class Char : MonoBehaviour {
6     public float Speed = 5f;
7
8     void Start () {
9
10    }
11
12
13    void FixedUpdate () {
14        if (Input.GetKey(KeyCode.W))
15        {
16            transform.position += Vector3.forward * Time.deltaTime * Speed; }
17
18        }
19
20        }
21
22
23
```

Figure 4-6: The movement code.

The next difference in the code shows what exactly `Speed` is affecting. Below `void Start`, you should add `void FixedUpdate(){`, which will update the code every second as opposed to every frame. Inside the `FixedUpdate`, you should type **if (Input. GetKey(KeyCode.W)) {**.

The `if` tells the game that the following string will happen only if the statement in the parentheses happens. In this example, when the player inputs a particular key on the keyboard, with that key defined by the KeyCode as `w`, than the following code happens:

```
transform.position += Vector3.forward *
         Time.deltaTime * Speed; }
```

The code indicates that the object, when clicked, will

- transform (change) its position by +=
  (a distance in a direction).

REMEMBER

All parentheses and brackets have to be closed. Otherwise, they'll register as broken codes. Every time you see an open bracket or parenthesis, try to find where it closes. If you can't find one, then close it. Keep in mind that if you have multiple strings, the brackets within the bracket must all be closed before the top bracket can be closed.

- The direction is indicated by `Vector3` as a direction on the XYZ axis. (`Vector2` indicates only along the 2D axis.)

- `.forward` determines which way the object is moving. It's moving forward relative to its direction multiplied by `Time.deltaTime * Speed`, which you defined earlier as 5.

The final code should look like this:

```
FixedUpdate {
(Input.GetKey (KeyCode.W)) {
     transform.position += Vector3.forward * Time.
deltaTime * Speed; }
}
```

So your character is moving 5 units forward along the XYZ axis whenever the W button is pressed. To get your character to move every direction, you must simply copy the pre-existing code and alter it as necessary for the different directions. See Figure 4-7 for an example.

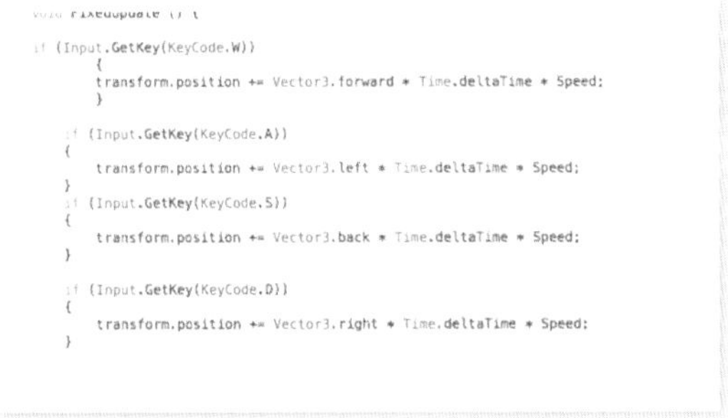

```
      FixedUpdate () {
if (Input.GetKey(KeyCode.W))
        {
        transform.position += Vector3.forward * Time.deltaTime * Speed;
        }
    if (Input.GetKey(KeyCode.A))
    {
        transform.position += Vector3.left * Time.deltaTime * Speed;
    }
    if (Input.GetKey(KeyCode.S))
    {
        transform.position += Vector3.back * Time.deltaTime * Speed;
    }
    if (Input.GetKey(KeyCode.D))
    {
        transform.position += Vector3.right * Time.deltaTime * Speed;
    }
```

Figure 4-7: All the directions.

The only parts of the code that you need to fix are the keys pressed and the directions that the character will be moving. Everything else is predefined and has no need to be adjusted:

- `KeyCode.A plus Vector3.Left` causes the character to move left when A is pressed.

- `KeyCode.S plus Vector3.Back` causes the character to move back when S is pressed.

- `KeyCode.D plus Vector3.Right` causes the character to move right when D is pressed.

After finishing this part of the code, you should save and go back to Unity to test it. To attach the code to a character, simply click and drag the code from the Project window over to your character on the Scene window. Once the code is attached, all you need to do is press Play, and you'll be able to move your character around.

If an error message appears, check your code and make sure that you're using the correct punctuation, you're capitalizing only in the noted areas, and that all the brackets are closed. Generally most errors in codes come from one or two simple spelling errors or misplaced punctuation marks. When an error occurs, Unity and MonoDevelop will refer to what line and column the error is occurring in, which can help you determine the exact problem.

After the basic movement code is complete, the next part of the code you'll be working on is the jump code (see Figure 4-8). Jump codes are actually very similar to your standard movement code. The only difference is that, because your character has the Rigidbody component, gravity will be acting opposite of this movement. As Isaac Newton put it, what goes up must come down.

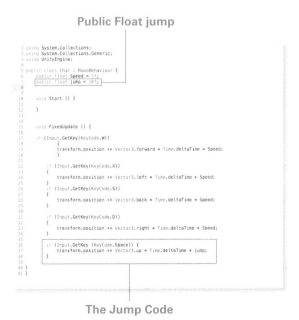

Figure 4-8: The jump code.

The first thing you need to do for the jump code is define another float for the jump to go off of. You can use the `Speed` float to adjust the height of your jump, or to change how fast the character is moving, but it's important that you can do so without changing the other. So first, you'll create a new `public float` and give it the name `jump`:

```
public float jump = 10f;
```

> Note that the `jump` name's first letter is lowercase and the `Speed` name's first letter is uppercase. It doesn't matter whether you use uppercase or lowercase when naming your floats — the names act as placeholders for a specific value. That said, whatever casing you do use needs to remain consistent for the name throughout the rest of the code, or the computer will not recognize it. When you're coding your own project, I suggest you pick a certain casing scheme (camel case is the most common for coding) so that you won't need to double-check that you're using the proper casing.

REMEMBER

Camel case is when two or more words are put together without spacing and the different sections of the word are indicated by an uppercase letter (like camelCase).

Set the float integer to 10f to make it double the base movement, and give the character a solid jump height so that they can clear the gaps created in your level and eventually, the enemies you'll create later in this book. Next, you have to reference the float later in the code and define when and how it will be used.

The code for the jump is the same code you used for the other movement codes, but you'll need to change the *keycode* (which key on the keyboard it uses) and the `Vector3` direction. For the keycode, the common jump key for most computer games is the Spacebar, so you'll be using that in your game. (Make sure that the S is capitalized.) As for the direction, this will cause the character to move simply use the direction "up." This will create a simple jump code that will allow the character to jump. Save your code and test it in your game. You'll notice that the character's jump is really high, so go back into the code and change the float integer to 5f:

```
(Input.GetKey(KeyCode.Space)) {
    transform.position += Vector3.up
* Time.deltaTime * jump; }
```

REMEMBER

Save your scene
and project.

CODING ADVANCED MOVEMENT

After you finish your basic movement codes, it's time to create codes to allow your character to sprint and to prevent your character from double jumping or just continuously floating. These may seem like small adjustments, but a simple sprint code can go a long way toward improving a player's enjoyment.

Starting with the top of the code in Figure 4-9, you'll notice that another float has been added along with two `public bool`s. The new float, `SSpeed`, represents the sprinting speed in your game. The way you'll be coding your game, this sprint speed will be added to your normal speed when your character is moving. The `bool`s operate in a similar way to the floats, but unlike the floats, `bool`s only have two possible values: `true` and `false`. Set both `bool`s to false and the `SSpeed` to 10f.

Sprint Float **GroundTouch bools**

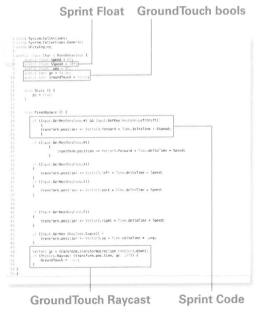

GroundTouch Raycast **Sprint Code**

Figure 4-9: Advanced movement code.

The next change to the code is within the void Start. Inside the void Start, the code refers back to one of the bools, gc, and changes its value from false to true, which will directly relate to a later part of the code, indicating that that part of the code should begin when the game is started.

In the FixedUpdate string you made earlier, a new if statement relating to the W keycode has been added. The code is similar to the first code you made, with one major difference: There is a second Input indicated in this code.

If you ever need to have multiple aspects acting on a string at once or multiple parts that need to be referenced for a string to work properly, you can do so by adding a && to the code in between the two parts. In this case, in order to activate the if statement, two buttons need to be pressed on the keyboard: W and LeftShift. So you define each keycode normally, but in order to link the two together you include them in the same parenthesis next to the if statement and link them with &&. The other change to this code is minimal because all it does is simply replace the Speed float with the SSpeed. You'll notice that the basic forward movement also remains unchanged after this string. That's because you want to keep the player's ability to sprint and to move both possible but separate. Only the forward sprint was added to this part of the code, but to add sprinting to every direction simply use the same base of the code and apply it to each of the directions. Here's an example:

```
(Input.GetKey(KeyCode.W) &&
         (Input.GetKey(KeyCode.LeftShift)) {
    transform.position += Vector3.forward *
         Time.deltaTime * SSpeed;
}
```

The final change to the code is at the very bottom of the code and refer-ences the bools. This code prevents the object from being able to double jump (or remain floating when holding the Spacebar) by using a raycast. Raycasts cast a ray out from a specific part of the object in a direction to measure if there are any colliders nearby. If a raycast is set to 10f in the forward direction, then when a collider is measured that is 10 units in front of the object, the raycast will pick it up. This can be used to create messages that warn of colliders nearby or trigger an interaction between the two objects. Think of trainer battles in Pokémon. When you pass a certain distance in front of a trainer in Pokémon, a battle begins. This prevents you from needing to adjust the collider size of the object and instead note the distance between two objects. In this case, the raycast indicates when your object is touching the ground and prevents your character from jumping when the character is not within that distance from the ground:

```
Vector3 gc = transform.TransformDirection (Vector3.down);
if (Physics.Raycast (transform.position, gc, .5f)) {
GroundTouch = true;
}
```

First, the code indicates the direction the raycast is pointing with the gc's direction being transformed to the Vector3 direction down. This tells the raycast that the direction that it should be measuring in is down, which will point it toward the ground. Next, in the if statement, physics gives us access to raycast. It's considered a physics code, and from there the code defines how far the raycast is stretching. In this code, the raycast is stretching, along the gc, .5F (or half a unit). When that distance is measured, the code indicates that the character is touching the ground. Save your code and test it in Unity (see Figure 4-10). See if you can pick up the objects.

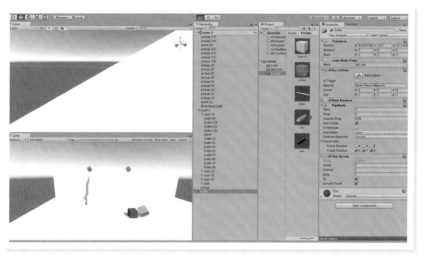

Figure 4-10: The character in Unity.

Something you may have noticed that hasn't yet been addressed is the new component in the Inspector window when you have your character selected. This component is the script you just made, but you'll also notice that the names of the floats and bools you made are available to alter here as well. Part of making the floats public gives you the ability to alter these values even outside of the code. This is useful because it allows you to adjust your character's speed, jump distance, and sprinting speed during testing. The only thing you have to remember when doing so is that any changes you make to these numbers while your game is running will not be recorded. You must not be in play mode when making these changes.

Now as you play the game, you'll also notice that your character is not picking up the items you made in Chapter 3 for the character to pick up. That's because you haven't created a code for the character to pick up the items yet. All they're acting as right now are objects that the character can bump into while the character is going through the level. Now it's time for you to add a pickup code and point system into your level.

This would also be a good time to change the name of cube to Player so that you can better recognize it right away when working within Unity.

CODING PICKUP

Collectables are simple ways to indicate a goal in your game. Attaching numerical value to the items will help reinforce the idea that players should pick up the items. Unfortunately, your code has no way to express that the player is doing anything as of right now. In order to give the code the ability to alter text on a screen, you must first give it control over the user interface (UI) in the game.

Underneath where the code accesses the Unity engine, add `using UnityEngine.UI;` (see Figure 4-11). This will give the code the ability to alter any UI you add to your game, which will allow it to print messages to the player as well as indicate the player's score.

```
1 using System.Collections;
2 using System.Collections.Generic;
3 using UnityEngine;
4 using UnityEngine.UI;
5
```

Figure 4-11: The code for accessing the Unity UI.

Now part of the pickup code is not only to allow your character to pick up the objectives but also to have the objective disappear when it collides with your character and for the UI to indicate an increase to a "score" that will increase by one every time your character passes through any of the objectives. That's a lot to code. To make it easier, I'll break this code into two halves: the beginning of the code where you define the text and integers that will be affected by the code and change, as well as setting up the beginning of the count, and the end of the code where you define how and why those text and integers change and how they relate to each other.

At the top of your code (see Figure 4-12) is where you previously added floats and bools. You'll be adding two new types of codes that will be affecting your game and other parts of your code:

public Text

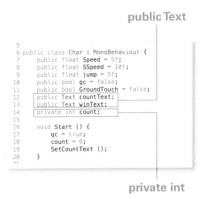

private int

Figure 4-12: The beginning of the code.

- **Text:** Text codes relate directly to the UI and are determined in the code. These can be simple messages that appear during the game or even values that change as things happen in the game.

- **int:** int codes are integers. They're number codes that are determined during the code and increase or decrease in value depending on the code that you write. These can be used to define a countdown clock or a point system.

You'll also notice that while both the texts are public (which means that their values are broadcasted outside of the code to other aspects of the game or codes), the int code is private, which means its value is only used within this particular code and does not affect other parts of the game.

The text codes that you want to make are countText and winText. Similar to the floats, the names here don't actually matter beyond their value as an indication of a further code. These codes will be used to count the player's score, and once the player has hit a certain score indicates that the player has "won" the game.

You want to name the int code `count`. Again, the name doesn't matter, but `count` will indicate to you or any other person who looks at this code that this integer is directly relating to counting something. In this case, the integer is counting the amount of pickup items that the player has collected.

After you add these codes, go down to the `void Start` string where you'll add two new codes:

- `Count = 0;:` This will set the count integer to zero at the beginning of the level. After setting it to zero, you'll be able to make the number increase later during the code.

- `SetCountText ();:` This code refers to the text code you'll have later. After every integer change, this code will record the change and send it to the text code to change its number accordingly.

At the bottom of the code (see Figure 4-13), two voids have been added in the `void FixedUpdate: void OnTriggerEnter (Collider other)` and `void SetCountText ():`

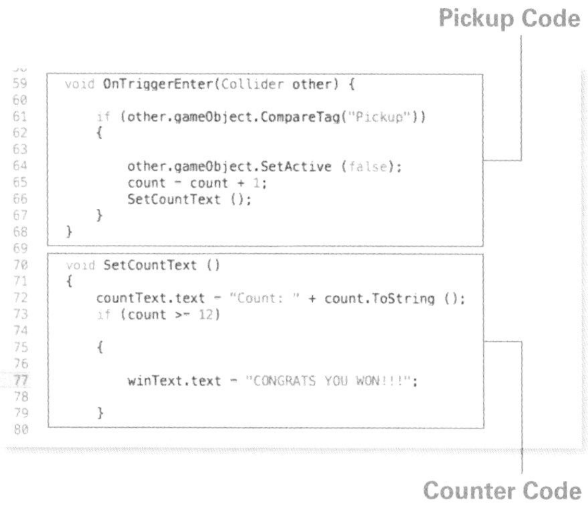

Pickup Code

```
59    void OnTriggerEnter(Collider other) {
60
61        if (other.gameObject.CompareTag("Pickup"))
62        {
63
64            other.gameObject.SetActive (false);
65            count - count + 1;
66            SetCountText ();
67        }
68    }
69
70    void SetCountText ()
71    {
72        countText.text - "Count: " + count.ToString ();
73        if (count >- 12)
74
75        {
76
77            winText.text - "CONGRATS YOU WON!!!";
78
79        }
80
```

Counter Code

Figure 4-13: The end of the code.

```
Void OnTriggerEnter (Collider other) {
    If (other.gameObject.CompareTag("Pickup")
    {
```

```
        other.gameObject.SetActive (false);
        count = count + 1;
        Set CountText ();
    }
}
```

The `onTriggerEnter` only activates when a certain event happens, in the parentheses that event is defined when the object's collider is in contact with another collider. What that means is whenever the character touches another object, this code begins to run, but to limit this code to only affect the pickup items within this string is an `if` statement: `if (other.gameObject.CompareTag("Pickup"))`. So now the code has determined that whenever the object collides with another, if that other object's tag is `Pickup`, the next part of the string happens.

The first line in this part of the string indicates that when this collides with the other object, it will change its `SetActive` to `false`. This will cause the other object to disappear in the game, making it look like it was picked up when in reality it's just no longer being rendered in the game. The next line sets our count integer to `count + 1`, which increases the total count by 1. Finally, in the third line, the code resets the `countText` with the integer.

Now whenever the game character touches an object with the `Pickup`, that object will disappear and the player's score will increase by 1.

`SetCountText ()` has already been referred to multiple times in this code. This string does define what happens when `SetCountText` is referred to. Inside this string, the code refers back to the `countText` public text that was set up earlier.

`countText.text = "Count: " + count.ToString ();`

This will define the `countText` and tell a user interface (UI) what to text to display. You determine that this is a text file and, thus, has words that have to be defined. Within the quotation marks, you specify the words that `countText` will display and indicate that it will also include the integer count at the end of the words. By adding the `+`, the computer knows to add the integer to the end of the stated phrase. Because every time the character picks up an object the code refers back to this string, the value at the end of the string will grow as you collect more items.

At the very end of `SetCountText()` is an `if` statement that determines when to display `winText`. When count is equal to or greater than 12, the `winText` will display the message "CONGRATS YOU WON!!!" This value can differ depending on the amount of pickup items you have scattered throughout the level, but the code will work regardless of the exact number. Just change the number to match how many pickup items are on the level. Here's the finished code:

```
void SetCountText ()
  {
     countText.text = "count: " + count.ToString;
     if (count >= 12)
  {

     winText.text = "CONGRATS YOU WON!!!"
}

}
```

Save the code, and return to Unity to test it out (see Figure 4-14).

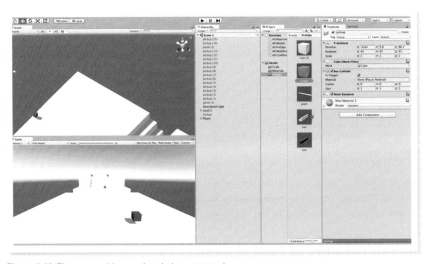

Figure 4-14: The game with completed character code.

REMEMBER

Save your scene and project.

As of right now, the code will not work because you have yet to set up a UI interface and create a tag that will allow the pickup items to be collected.

CREATING TAGS AND A USER INTERFACE

The code works fine, but the problem is that the game has no way to recognize the code. There is no UI for the code to change and nothing that will make the pickup items recognize that the code is referring to them.

CREATING A USER INTERFACE

Creating a UI is actually very simple. Like any other game object simply go to GameObject, scroll down to UI, and select Text. This will create a canvas with text on it. Where the canvas is and how large it is don't matter because the UI is automatically fitted into the camera's view. The text settings do matter, though.

First, in the Inspector window, change the name of the text to `Count Text` so that you can easily find it when you need to link the UI to the code. Next, the goal is to have the count text in the upper-left corner of the screen, so first adjust the position to (X=0,Y=0,Z=0). At the upper left of the Inspector, there will be an anchor point indicator. Click that indicator and select the upper-left corner and then move the position so that the text will be seen on the upper left of the game window. In my game, X = 95, Y = –34, and Z = 0, but this could different for your game. Toward the bottom of the Inspector window, you'll see some basic text settings that will change the color, size, and font of the text. Find what works best for your game. Click the Best Fit box, which will fit the text to the screen to make it as readable as possible without covering too much of the actual screen. Don't worry about the actual text because your code will replace text when it connects to the UI.

After you finish creating this UI, create another UI and name it `Win Text`. Instead of placing it toward the left corner, center it and make sure it's bold and italic (select the font style and select bold and italic). Also click Best Fit for this one, but change its maximum size to 60 and it minimum size to 10. Finally, delete all the text in this box because while the text will replace this text, it will not do so until the end, so having it empty will make sure that the game window is empty until you win.

Now that you created the UI, you have to link the text on the UI to your code. Luckily Unity makes this very simple.

1. **Select your player.**

2. **Scroll down on the Inspector until you reach your Char (Script) component.**

3. **Select the target next to Count Text.**

   A Select Text pop-up window will appear.

4. **Select Count Text.**

5. **Repeat for Win Text (selecting Win Text instead).**

This will attach the UI to your code and will make it so that the UI text will be changed by the code.

CREATING A TAG

Tags are references that can be assigned to one or more game objects. Used with codes, tags can help determine things like certain items being able to be picked up or enemies being able to destroy the character on contact. It's a way to assign a value to multiple objects at once. Earlier in this chapter, you already defined a tag that will be affected by our character, Pickup. Now you have create that tag and assign it to the object you want the character to pick up.

To create a tag, simply click any object. In the upper left of the Inspector window, you'll see a Tag drop-down menu. Selecting this menu will show some already created tags that are in Unity:

- Untagged

- Respawn

- Finish

- EditorOnly

- MainCamera

- Player

- GameController

To create your own tag, scroll to the bottom of the tag list and select Add Tag. This will open up a Tags & Layers window. In this window, in the Tags drop-down, simply click the + to create a new tag and name it Pickup. This will create a Pickup tag.

If you create the wrong tag, simply select the tag and hit the – to delete it.

After you create this tag, go to the Prefabs folder and select your Pickup prefab. Assign it the tag Pickup, and save your scene and project.

Before you play your scene, in order for the collider to work properly, go to the box collider in the Inspector window and open the drop-down. Make sure that the box next to Trigger is checked; otherwise, nothing will happen when the character collides with the object.

Press Play to test out your game. Now whenever your character crosses paths with any of the pickups it will pick them up and the score will increase.

CODING YOUR CAMERA

The last thing you need to code for your game in this chapter is your camera. Right now, the camera just stays still as your character moves around the screen, but what you want the camera to do is follow your character around the level. To do this, you have to first create a new code specifically for your camera. Create a new C# code in your code folder and name it `Cam`. Then open that code up.

The camera code isn't as in depth as the character code (see Figure 4-15), but it still adds some new codes. The first five lines of the code remain the same and do not need to be changed. After the `public` class, you want to add a `public` and a `private`:

```
1 using System.Collections;
2 using System.Collections.Generic;
3 using UnityEngine;
4
5 public class Cam : MonoBehaviour {
6
7     public GameObject Player;
8
9     private Vector3 offset;
10
11
12     void Start () {
13         offset = transform.position - Player.transform.position;
14     }
15
16     void LateUpdate () {
17
18         transform.position = Player.transform.position + offset;
19
20     }
21 }
22
```

Figure 4-15: The camera code.

- `public GameObject Player;`: This gives the camera code the ability to select a particular object and determine its value as Player. It works similar to the text code created in the `char` code.

- `private Vector3 offset;:` This part of the code allows you to freely move around the camera in Unity to create the angle you want it to follow the player on. This way, in the code, you don't have to define what the distance and rotation is.

In the `void Start` string, write `offset = transform.position - Player.Transform.position;`. This will link the offset of the camera (how far away from its target it is) to the Player GameObject you created earlier. The transform position of the camera is directly linked to the position of the player from the start:

```
void Start () {
    offset = transform.position -
        Player.Transform.position;

}
```

In `void LateUpdate` (which will replace `void Update`), write `transform.position = Player.transform.position + offset;`. This will ensure that as the subject's position changes, the camera's offset will update every second of the game. That way the camera will always be the exact same distance away from the character.

```
void LateUpdate () {
    transform.position = Player.transform.position
        + offset;
}
```

In this code, you determine what the camera is following, how it follows the character, and what the offset is.

Save the code and return to Unity.

After you finish the code, simply drag and drop it onto the Camera in the scene window. The camera won't start following the character just yet because you still have to determine within Unity the character that the camera is following and the angle/distance at which it follows the character.

Select the camera and scroll to the bottom of the Inspector where you'll see Cam (Script) component. Inside the component, you'll see Player with a target next to it. Select the target, and a window listing all the objects in the scene will pop up. Scroll until you find Player and select it. Save your scene and project and press Play. Now when you move your character, the camera will follow behind the player (see Figure 4-16).

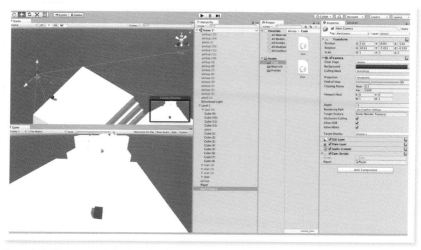

Figure 4-16: The camera following the character at an angle.

After you finish setting up the camera to follow the player, adjust the angle of the camera using the position and rotation transformations to best follow your character while providing the best view of the level.

Having the camera be above the character at a slight angle works best in 3D platformers.

CHAPTER

05

Making Your "Game" into a Game

In this chapter, you'll create obstacles for players to avoid, as well as code negative effects that will happen when the player *doesn't* avoid these obstacles. The obstacles you create here will act as stand-ins for more detailed enemies or traps that you'll add in Chapter 12.

You'll also program a death message that will appear when the character dies. You'll set up a limit to how far the character can fall before being forced to respawn. You'll learn how to program the character to relocate to a spawn point after it dies from falling, as well as how to set up multiple spawn points in a level.

THINKING ABOUT WHAT A GAME IS

What makes a game a game? A game is only a game when there is some sense of *challenge* to it. There has to be a goal and an obstacle. Even games as open-ended as Minecraft have a sense of purpose and a type of challenge to them. The purpose of Minecraft is to build and explore, and the challenge is finding the right materials to use and surviving against creatures. Games need challenge to draw interest. If a game has no challenge or goal, it ceases to be a game and is just an application.

As an exercise, think of three games that you play, and write down what the goal of each game is and what's preventing you from achieving that goal. In multiplayer games, this challenge becomes other players. In puzzle games, it's the puzzle that you have to solve. And in choice-based story games, the challenge is trying to figure out what options will lead to the outcome you want.

When you create your game, ask yourself what type of obstacle will prevent the player from reaching her goal and how the player can overcome this obstacle. In the game that you're making in this book, the obstacle takes the form of enemy characters and spikes that the player can't hit without losing health and dying.

CHALLENGING VERSUS PUNISHING

Why is a game like Super Meat Boy fun? The game's difficulty is grueling, and the levels require near perfect timing to complete. Despite how challenging the game is, it never crosses into punishing. This is mainly due to its near-instantaneous respawn time in each level. Before you can even realize how you died, you're already back to playing the game.

Death doesn't hurt the flow of the game. This is one of the key reasons why Super Meat Boy was as successful as it was. If every time you died in Super Meat Boy you were forced to wait just 10 seconds to respawn, the game's difficulty would no longer add to the fun of the game. Instead, the difficulty would detract from it. Games have to be challenging enough to feel rewarding when accomplished while not being so difficult or punishing as to make them feel tedious.

The line between challenging and punishing is thin. Keep that line in mind whenever you design your levels or challenges. This doesn't mean that games can't be difficult or even punish players harshly for their mistakes, but it does mean that as a designer you have to understand how you can keep a player interested in a game even when the difficulty begins to spike. Super Meat Boy does this by never making the respawn time too long so that players never feel punished for making a mistake, even when later levels ramp up the difficulty of the game. Games like Dark Souls, which are famous for their difficulty, never punish players without giving them ample warning or hints that something will happen. The game's challenge is in finding those subtle hints and learning to recognize them throughout the game. As discussed in Chapter 3, many games get away with extremely difficult levels because of natural progression inside and outside of the game. Players learn and apply what they learn from one level to the next.

When you make your game, you have to think about how you can progress your player slowly enough that they don't hit a wall during play that they can't overcome, but fast enough that they don't get bored. Games thrive on challenge. Players appreciate failure — to some degree. Games teach players about failure and offer tools to learn from those failures. Players don't hate failing — they hate being punished unevenly. If a punishment is too harsh for the mistake, it alienates players. But if it's too tame, it bores them. Consider this when making the obstacles and respawns for your game.

CREATING AND CODING YOUR OBSTACLES

Now that you've completed the basic controls and layout for your level (see Figure 5-1), you need to add something that can give players a challenge to overcome.

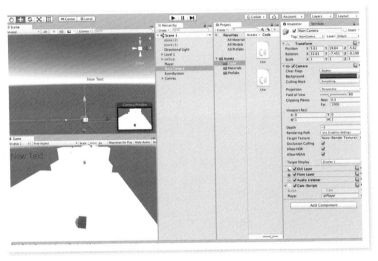

Figure 5-1: Your level.

You already have gaps for them to leap over, but that's different from an actual obstacle. Like a Goomba in Super Mario Bros. or a spike trap, you should have things in your game that players have to avoid or overcome. Enemies are probably the simplest version of this concept, so that's what you're going to make.

As has become a pattern in the early levels of the game, you should start off with a stand-in that you can add the code to and that you can replace later with the more polished game object. You need to make sure that the code and placement work properly before you spend time and effort on an animation or model. In this case,

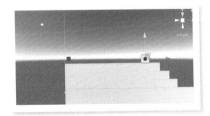

Figure 5-2: Placing the enemy stand-in.

start by creating a cube and placing it near the first platform's edge (see Figure 5-2).

The problem with this stand-in is that, like the original pickup stand-ins, the enemy character doesn't stand out from the background. So, before you even make a prefab of the enemy, you should change the color of the character so it stands out from the background. A color that works well for an enemy character is red because of people's natural association of the color red with anger and the word *stop*. Most people see red as a dangerous color, so using it as the enemy color — at least for the stand-in — can help indicate that it's bad and should be avoided.

Another thing you can do to make the enemy seem dangerous is to make it larger. This serves two purposes:

- It creates a larger object that the character will have to avoid.

- It makes the character stand out and seem imposing.

A scale of (X=2,Y=2,Z=2) should be enough to create a simple stand-in that you can later replace with a moving enemy.

Finally, be sure to assign this object a tag that you can later use in the code to indicate that it has negative conse- quence. Create a new tag and name it enemy. After you assign the tag to the character, make sure that the Trigger box is checked off in the box collider and make a prefab for the character. When you're done, you should have some- thing that looks similar to Figure 5-3.

Figure 5-3: The finished enemy stand-in.

Save your project/scene and open your Char code.

Whenever you code, ask yourself what exactly you want your code to do. The best way to code is to go in understanding what you want out of the code. As of right now, your character code gives your player the ability to

- Move in four directions

- Jump

- Pick up items

- Sprint

- Count how many items you've picked up

- Display a win message when you've collected a certain number of items

Now you want to add code that gives the character the ability to recognize when it runs into an enemy, have its score reduced by 1 every time it touches an enemy, bounce back away from the enemy when it hits it, and die when it runs into an enemy with a score of 0.

Codes are like blocks — they build off of each other. As you code more in the future, ask yourself what problem each piece of code solves and how it relates to the rest of the code. Memorizing codes can be helpful, but understanding the meaning behind each code can help you more creatively use coding in the future. There is no one solution for any coding problem. Sometimes a single solution can work for multiple problems.

To start, create a float that determines how far back the character will go when it runs into an enemy. It should be more than any of the other speeds so that when a player accidentally runs into an enemy, she doesn't accidentally do it twice. As in Figure 5-4, name this float hurt and give it a value of 30f.

```
1 using System.Collections;
2 using System.Collections.Generic;
3 using UnityEngine;
4 using UnityEngine.UI;
5
6 public class Char : MonoBehaviour {
7     public float Speed = 5f;
8     public float SSpeed = 10f;
9     public float jump = 5f;
10    public float hurt = 30f;
11    public bool gc = false;
12    public bool GroundTouch = false;
13    public Text countText;
14    public Text winText;
15    private int count;
```

Figure 5-4: The upper half of the code.

```
Public float hurt = 30f;
```

This value may have to be adjusted later when you're testing the game, but for now it will act as a good placeholder value because it's larger than any of the other values.

Now it's time to write the code for what happens when your character bumps into an enemy character (see Figure 5-5). This code should be placed in the void OnTriggerEnter (Collider other) section of the code. Similar to the `pickup` code, the first part of this code tells the player that when he crosses an object with the tag `Enemy`, the following event will happen.

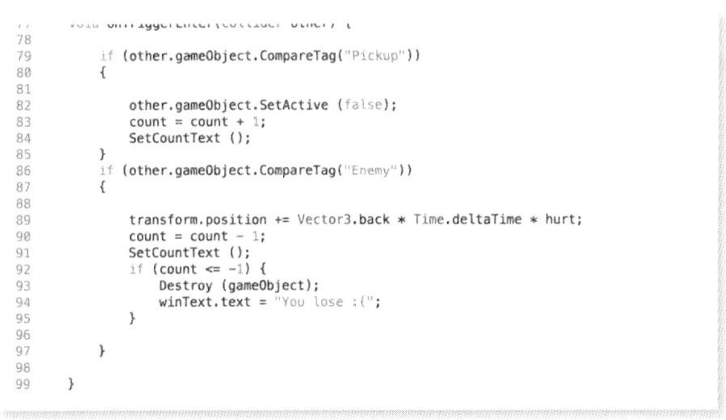

```
        if (other.gameObject.CompareTag("Pickup"))
        {

            other.gameObject.SetActive (false);
            count = count + 1;
            SetCountText ();
        }
        if (other.gameObject.CompareTag("Enemy"))
        {

            transform.position += Vector3.back * Time.deltaTime * hurt;
            count = count - 1;
            SetCountText ();
            if (count <= -1) {
                Destroy (gameObject);
                winText.text = "You lose :(";
            }

        }

    }
```

Figure 5-5: The lower half of the code.

```
If (other.gameObject.CompareTag("Enemy")){
transform.position += Vector3.back * Time.deltaTime *
   Hurt;
count = count - 1;
SetCountText ();
if (count <= -1) {
     Destroy (gameObject);
     winText.text = "You lose :(";
}
}
```

Thinking back to the movement codes, you don't need to limit events that change the position of the character to just pressing keys on the keyboard. In this case, whenever your character touches an enemy, the character's position is transformed backward by `hurt`, which you defined in Figure 5-4. You can test this code by saving and playing your game in Unity. When you run into the enemy, your character will now jump back.

But you want to do more than push a character back. The next part of this string determines the consequence of running into a character.

In Chapter 4, you defined that whenever the character picks up one of the pickup items, its `score` increases by 1. You're going to link that score to the player's `health`. Every time the character hits enemy, the character loses 1 point. If those points go below 0, the player loses the game.

The code itself is fairly straightforward. It's the opposite of the `pickup` code in Chapter 4:

- Instead of the `Count = Count + 1`, the code changes to `Count = Count - 1` so that the count goes down every time the character hits the enemy.

- `SetCounntText()` remains the same because every time this happens you want the count to change on the screen.

- Add another `if` statement within the code so that when the character runs into the enemy, if its score is equal to or less than –1, the character is destroyed and the `winText` UI displays "You Lose" instead of "You Win."

- `Destroy()` removes something from the game when it's activated. In this case, it removes `gameObject`, which refers to the object the code is attached to.

With the exception of `Destroy`, no code within this `if` statement was new. They were all codes you used in previous parts that accomplish different goals.

Don't be afraid to reuse codes. Coding is deceptive in its simplicity. It looks far more intimidating than it actually is, but when you know the core of the language, you can do anything!

The problem with using the pickup items as a way to measure health is that you can't have the goal of the level be to pick up a certain number of them because if the player loses too much health, there is no way for them to complete the level. To rectify this problem, add a clearer objective at the end of the level for the player to reach. Similar to the flag at the end of a Mario level or the sign at the end of the Sonic level, there has to be something that marks the end of the level for the player and tells the game that the level is over.

This can be a flag or a special-looking pickup item, but for the purposes of coding ease, just add a new tag and name it `Finish`. Then follow these steps to create an endpoint like the one in Figure 5-6:

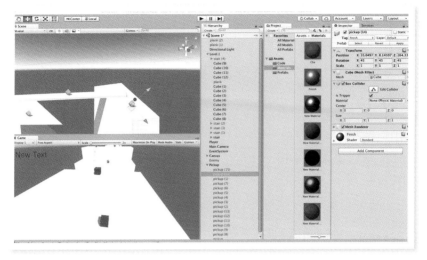

Figure 5-6: The end point.

1. Place a `pickup` prefab at the very end of the level.

2. Create a new material and change its color.

   Gold works well.

3. Assign the new material to the new pickup.

4. Change the tag of this pickup to `Finish`.

At this point, your level has a lot of different game objects in the level and your hierarchy can feel crowded. An easy solution is to create some empties that you can parent your objects to by type. This way, you can organize your hierarchy without worrying too much about where everything is. You want to parent it to a new empty — this is just for organization, so you don't want to link different objects together that may have codes that could interfere with each other. For example, if you parent all the pickup items to a single one, when that one is picked up, the rest will disappear. Using an empty as the parent will prevent this from happening. Be sure to name the empties.

After you create the `finish` object, you still have to code the character so that when they cross the Finish, they actually display the victory message.

When programing the end code (like the one in Figure 5-7), you need to first delete your original `winText` code that you had in an `if` statement in the `SetCountText ()`. Instead, write out an `if` statement similar to your `pickup` and `enemy` codes but instead for `Finish`. Then write out the code to display the `winText` that was used in `SetCountText`. Now when your character crosses the finish line, the game will display the text "CONGRATS YOU WON!!!" As with the other codes with `CompareTag`, this should be in the collider section of the code.

Figure 5-7: The end code.

```
If (other.gameObject.CompareTag
    ("Finish"))
{
winText.text = "CONGRATS YOU WON!!!";
}
```

REMEMBER

Save your project and scene.

After testing out your game and making sure that the codes work, use the enemy prefab created earlier in the chapter and begin placing them throughout your level. Although these characters don't move right now, give them space to move for when you animate the enemies later. After adding a few enemies, you should also make a new box at the end of the level and give it the red material. For this one, though, make the box spread across the entire platform so that the player has no choice but to jump over it. This object will act as a placeholder for a large trap in the level. Instead of an enemy, this one represents a spike trap or a similar environmental hazard the player has to avoid. Create a new tag and name it EnviroHazard03. (This will be a hazard in the third respawn point section.)

Make sure that the trap is avoidable. In Figure 5-8, the trap's height is only 1. That way, the player has the ability to jump over it easily. In the final game, this trap will be a crushing trap that the player will have to jump through before it crushes down, but right now the trap should act as something the player can easily avoid. When the player runs into it, he'll will be forced to respawn.

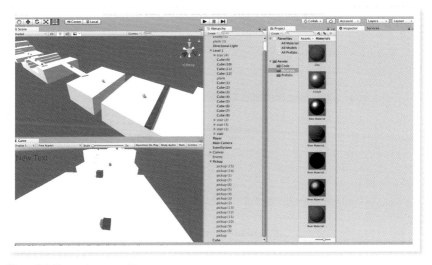

Figure 5-8: The environmental trap.

CREATING RESPAWN POINTS

Why create respawn points? If a player has to start from the beginning of the level every time she falls off the edge or loses a life, the game isn't fun and just becomes frustrating. Having to do the same thing over and over again just to get back to the point that was challenging can aggravate a player and break immersion. Have you ever played a game and gotten to a difficult boss fight that has an unskippable cutscene in front of it? It's aggravating because you have to sit through the same cutscene over and over just to get an attempt at the boss again. The cutscene in Figure 5-9 is just one example of many games that have done this.

Figure 5-9: Kingdom Hearts HD 1.5 Remix: Riku/Ansem boss fight cutscene.

If you ever make a game with a cutscene, give the player the ability to skip the cutscene. If the story is good enough, the player won't choose to skip the cutscene, but it prevents a lot of frustration on the part of the player.

Respawn points act as a reprieve to such frustrations — they lessen the punishment for failure by making it so that the player has to go through less of the level. Many games, especially ones with long levels, have some sort of respawn point within the game so that players don't have to redo entire levels over and over again. These come in the form of automatic respawn points that appear when the player gets a certain distance into the level or save points that players can use to save their progress into the level or game.

For the purposes of your game, use the former method of respawn for your levels. These respawn points will be where players spawn after they fall off the edge of the level or hit an environmental hazard. They'll remove a coin similar to the enemies but will also not work if a player falls off the edge or hits an environmental hazard when they're at zero health because that will result in a game over.

Now, before creating the actual spawn points, you should give an indication to the player as to the location of the spawn points so that he has an idea of where he'll respawn when he falls off an edge or hits a hazard. In Figure 5-10, this is represented by changing the color of a platform where the respawn will be placed. I suggest having one or two respawn points within a level, depending on how long the level is, with more added in even longer levels. For level 1, there are two respawn points.

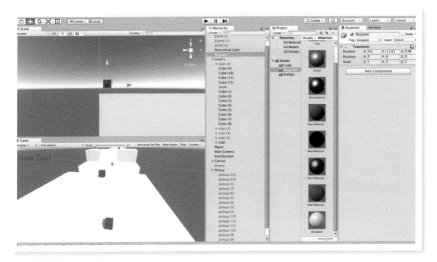

Figure 5-10: Respawn indication.

Changing a color or adding some sort of marker to a spot can help indicate to the player that there is a respawn point there and guide the player toward it. It also serves another purpose in giving the player some smaller objectives throughout the game that they can aim to reach for, especially when the actual objective may not even be in sight of the player.

After you determine the location of the two respawn points, it's time to start making the actual points that the character will respawn to. When creating a respawn point, you need two things: a trigger and a target.

- **Trigger:** In this case, a trigger is what causes the character to need to respawn. In games, this could be enemies or a zone outside the game area that, when a player crosses, causes the player to respawn. In this game, the triggers you'll set up will activate when the player falls off the edge of the level.

- **Target:** Targets are the actual respawn points that the character will spawn at. These are

REMEMBER

The goal of level 1 is to encourage and teach the player about the game. Slowly introducing the player to the game and giving some easy, small objectives in the game can help encourage the player to learn and move forward in the game.

objects or spots that the player is moved to when the player dies or falls off the edge. In the level, despite the fact that you have only two noticeable respawn points, to the player there will actually be three targets for respawn: two at the locations previously determined and one at the very start of the level. If a character falls off an edge before reaching the first respawn, the character spawns back to the beginning of the level. But like everything in game design, this also has to be coded; otherwise, it won't happen.

After indicating where you want the player to respawn to, it's time to place your respawn points around the level. I've found that the best game objects to use for respawn points are empties. Create three empties and name them Respawn. Place the respawn points in order in the level where you want the character to respawn to. See Figure 5-11 for an example of how and where to place the empties.

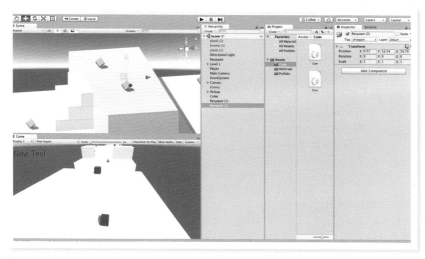

Figure 5-11: Placing your respawn points.

These respawn points will act as our targets that the character will be able to use as a reference for when he needs to respawn. The character when responding will copy the position of the empty and match it.

Next you have to set up triggers so that when the character falls off the edge of the map, they'll be forced to respawn instead of falling forever. For a trigger, I prefer to use a quad from the 3D Object menu. Follow these steps:

1. **Go to GameObject.**

2. **Scroll down to 3D Object.**

3. **Select Quad.**

   Any object would work for this, but the two best to use are quads and planes, and quads have less geometry to deal with, so I prefer to use them for the trigger.

4. **Rotate the quad 90 degrees on the *x*-axis.**

5. **Place the quad below the bottom of the level.**

6. **Size it so that part of the quad reaches to before the start of the level until it touches the area where you determined the first respawn point is.**

   The sides of the quad should stick out past the sides of the levels (see Figure 5-12).

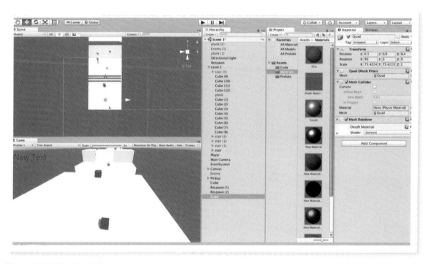

Figure 5-12: The first trigger.

You also want to make sure that the quad is invisible, so after you finish placing the mesh so that it matches or is similar to Figure 5-12, create a new material. Making an invisible material requires you to change the rendering mode the material uses. In the upper right of the Inspector window, when you make a new material, you'll see the Rendering

Mode drop-down menu. When you open that menu, you have four options:

- Opaque

- Fade

- Cutout

- Transparent

For the purposes of making an invisible object, I find that either Fade or Cutout works the best. Select one of those two and then select the Albedo color. When you select the Albedo, a color picker window pops up. At the bottom of the color picker window, you'll see four letters next to color sliders:

- R for Red

- G for Green

- B for Blue

- A for Alpha

Using the different color sliders allows you to change how much influence each color has, but Alpha determines how transparent or opaque (solid) an object is. This option is only available in the Fade, Cutout, or Transparent render settings.

REMEMBER

In order for the trigger to affect the character, you have to be sure that in the Inspector window, in the box collider component Is Trigger is checked.

Transparent doesn't work as well as the other two because it's more for rendering glass so it still has a glare. Dragging the Alpha all the way down to 0 will make the material completely invisible. After creating the material, assign it to the quad that you created, and now the quad will be invisible at the bottom of the level.

Name this quad DeathZone1 and save it. You want to create two more DeathZones and place one in between the two respawn points, and the other one from the last respawn point until just past the end of the level, as shown in Figure 5-13.

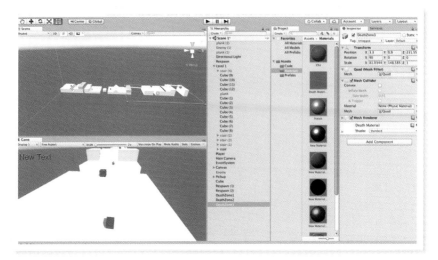

Figure 5-13: The first trigger.

There should be no empty space between any of the zones. This is to make sure that each respawn point has a corresponding zone that will spawn characters back to the respawn point. After you've created all the respawn points and zones, it's time to code them.

CODING RESPAWN POINTS

To code the respawn points, you'll use a slightly different system than you did for the other colliders. For one thing, instead of using tags, you'll instead be using a public GameObject.

At the top of the code, create six public GameObjects (see Figure 5-14), one for each trigger and target. The first three you should name death Zone01, deathZone02, and deathZone03; these will attach to the trigger zones created earlier in the chapter. Use the following as an example of how to write the code, replace the name for each one:

```
Public GameObject deathZone01;
```

The next three name respawnPoint1, respawnPoint2, and respawn Point3. These will target the respawn empties made earlier.

```
1 using System.Collections;
2 using System.Collections.Generic;
3 using UnityEngine;
4 using UnityEngine.UI;
5
6 public class Char : MonoBehaviour {
7     public float Speed = 5f;
8     public float SSpeed = 10f;
9     public float jump = 5f;
10     public float hurt = 30f;
11     public bool gc = false;
12     public bool GroundTouch = false;
13     public Text countText;
14     public Text winText;
15     private int count;
16     public GameObject deathZone01;
17     public GameObject deathZone02;
18     public GameObject deathZone03;
19     public GameObject respawnPoint1;
20     public GameObject respawnPoint2;
21     public GameObject respawnPoint3;
22
```

Figure 5-14: Public GameObjects.

In Chapter 4, you created a public GameObject to attach the camera to the player character. Public GameObjects allow you to choose specific targets that the code will affect. They can be useful if you want to have the same code for multiple levels because it's easy to target different objects for different levels. Thinking of it through respawn points, you want to be able to easily set up respawn points in every level, and tags don't work because each respawn needs to be coded individually so the fastest and most reliable way is to use GameObjects.

In Figure 5-15, you can see that the Respawn code itself is minimal, but you'll notice something that you haven't seen before. Instead of the usual `CompareTag` code that you've written before this code, you'll notice that the code has two equal signs.

```
115    if (other.gameObject == deathZone01) {
116        transform.position = respawnPoint1.transform.position;
117    }
```

Figure 5-15: The respawn code.

```
if (other.gameObject == deathZone01) {
transform.position = respawnPoint1.transform.position;
}
```

When the value is numerical, you only need to use one equal sign to say the object's value is equal to it, but for non-numerical instances — such as when the object collision has to match a certain object — it will require two equal signs for it to work properly.

In this `if` statement, if the other GameObject that is being touched is the `deathzone01` GameObject, then the position is transformed to match the position of the `respawnPoint1`. After finishing this code, save your file and switch to a Unity window to test out the code.

Select the player and go to the Inspector window. In the Char (Script) component, you'll now see a list of all the GameObjects you made in the code. Select the target next to Death Zone 01 and choose the first `DeathZone` that you created. Do the same for the respawn point (as shown in Figure 5-16). Save your scene and project and press Play. Now when your character falls off the edge of the level, it will respawn back at the start.

After you've tested the code and seen that it works, click the targets for the rest of the death zones and respawn points. Before you can test it, though, you'll need to repeat the same codes for the other targets and triggers.

Figure 5-16: Setting the GameObjects.

The only thing left to code for the falling respawn is the reduction to the total score count. For this, you just use the same code you made for the enemy codes. By setting this code up whenever the character falls off the edge, his score is reduced by 1 every time he respawns, and if he falls off the edge with no health, he will be destroyed. Coding this to happen is similar to the enemy codes before, setting it so that the count decreases by 1. If it goes under –1, it will end the game.

```
if (other.gameObject == deathZone01) {
transform.position = respawnPoint1.transform.position;
count = count - 1;
SetCountText ();
        if (count <=-1){
            Destroy (gameObject)
            winText.text = "You lose :(";
    }
    }
```

See Figure 5-17 for what the final code should look like.

Using this code as a basis you can also add a code for the environmental hazards. Instead of using the `if (other.gameObject ==` code, use the `CompareTag` code and copy the rest of the code from the `GameObject` codes. Make sure that the environmental hazard respawns to the third respawn point.

```
If (other.gameObject.CompareTag("EnviroHazard03")){
    transform.position = respawnPoint3.transform.position;
```

```
count = count - 1;
SetCountText ();
      if (count <=-1){
            Destroy (gameObject)
            winText.text = "You lose :(";
      }
}
```

```
:16      transform.position = respawnPoint1.transform.position;
:17      count = count - 1;
:18      SetCountText ();
:19      if (count <= -1) {
:20          Destroy (gameObject);
:21          winText.text = "You lose :(";
:22      }
:23    }
:24
:25      if (other.gameObject == deathZone02) {
:26          transform.position = respawnPoint2.transform.position;
:27          count = count - 1;
:28          SetCountText ();
:29          if (count <= -1) {
:30              Destroy (gameObject);
:31              winText.text = "You lose :(";
:32          }
:33      }
:34
:35      if (other.gameObject == deathZone03) {
:36          transform.position = respawnPoint3.transform.position;
:37          count = count - 1;
:38          SetCountText ();
:39          if (count <= -1) {
:40              Destroy (gameObject);
:41              winText.text = "You lose :(";
:42          }
:43      }
:44    }
```

Figure 5-17: The final respawn code.

After you finish coding the environmental hazards and the respawn points, you've finally completed your gray box level (see Figure 5-18). Save your scene and project.

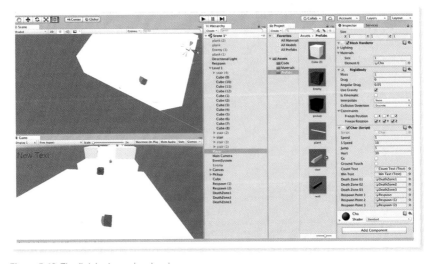

Figure 5-18: The finished gray box level.

CHAPTER

06

Play Testing

In this chapter, you'll play test your game for the first time. Play testing may be the hardest part of game design, especially for independent game developers who work by themselves or in a small team. It's hard for artists to show their work to someone for the first time with the sole purpose of getting criticism. People who have been artists or game developers for years *still* struggle with this fundamental part of art, so don't worry if it's hard for you. Putting your work out there is challenging.

This chapter helps you overcome some of the fears or mental blocks you may have when you think about play testing. This chapter also gives you some tips about what to look for whenever you test your game. No two games are the same, and no one set of answers exist for all games. The goal of this chapter is not to give you the answers for every game ever, but to give you the tools you'll need to better test your game in the future — and become a better game developer in the process!

DEFINING PLAY TESTING

When you think of play testing, the alpha or beta testers that developers bring in toward the latter half of the development cycle probably come to mind. You may think of play testers as people who are paid to play the game early and determine whether it's fun. But that's not all play testing is!

For one thing, play testers aren't just playing the game. They meticulously examine every part of the game and report any bugs or issues that come up. Play testers don't really even play the game. Instead, they dissect it to determine what works and what doesn't work on every level of the game.

As a game developer, you need to understand the importance of having a good play tester. When you look for play testers, you need to be sure that they're willing to not only play the game but take it apart piece by piece to determine what parts of the game work and what parts don't work.

Play testing isn't something to take lightly. When you play test your games, the purpose is to improve aspects of your game that may not be as developed as the others. Play testing is all about finding the parts of the game that aren't working and determine what exactly the game needs to fix — from bugs in the code to uneven spikes in the difficulty. Play testing is a stress test for your game. In play testing, you generally aren't examining the game as a whole. Instead, you're looking at individual aspects of the game as you play it. You'll probably want multiple play testers to help catch as many flaws within the game as possible.

KNOWING WHEN TO START PLAY TESTING

Play testing can never start too early. In fact, the earlier you begin to play test your game, the better off you'll be in the long run. Game development takes a lot of time and energy, and a lot of things depend on the different aspects of the game working together. Any one thing in the game requires multiple aspects of the game working at once to be sure that everything is going properly. The earlier you play test your game, and the more frequently you do so, the more it can help make sure that you don't have to redo entire sections of code or work just to fix one minor issue. The later in the game development a change is made, the more expensive and time consuming the mistake is. Something that would only take a few moments to fix in the early code can take hours or days to fix in a completed game.

Play testing shouldn't just happen early, it should happen often. If mistakes remain part of the code or design too long, the rest of the game begins to develop around those mistakes and interconnect other parts of the game to them. The more code or designs that are linked to a mistake, the longer and costlier the mistake becomes. Play testing is the only way to understand what works and what doesn't work about your game.

DECIDING WHO SHOULD PLAY TEST YOUR GAME

The hardest part about play testing is recognizing that you are your worst play tester. While you're designing your game, you make decisions based on what *you* would want to play. The problem with play testing your own game is that you go in knowing some of the problems in your game. You have blinders on about other problems and you're just looking for those problems — and missing others — from the start. You are your worst play tester — not because you don't understand what your game is doing, but because you understand it almost too well.

Think about your game like a story you're writing. When you write a story, you have a very clear idea of what that story is about. The characters all make sense to you, and their motivations are crystal clear because you wrote them. The problem that a lot of amateur writers run into is actually conveying those ideas on the page. This is why writers have editors. Just because something makes sense to you doesn't mean it will make sense to someone else. Game development is the same.

When you grab a play tester, ask yourself who you want to play your game. What's your target audience? Find friends or family members who match this description and let them play the game.

REMEMBER

Don't tell them anything about the game, not even the controls. Use this as a good chance to see if the controls come naturally or need to be added in.

After they finish playing, listen to what they tell you about your game. Make notes on what does and doesn't work or what they found confusing. What may seem obvious to you won't necessarily be obvious to them, and this is an important criticism because you want your game to be accessible to as many people as possible.

If possible, have multiple people test your game. The best thing you can do is test as many ages or demographics as possible, not just your target audience. Although you should take the criticisms of your target audience into heavier consideration, don't underestimate the advice of groups that are *not* your target. To make a game that people enjoy, you have to understand the importance of different perspectives.

Even if you decide that the criticism or suggestion is not what is best for your game, it's important to at least consider the suggestion. Even if you don't take the suggestion, you'll be forced to think about your game on a deeper level and understand more about what your game is and what you find is important. By using other people to test your game, questions will come up that you may never have even considered. There is no such thing as a bad question in game design.

KNOWING WHAT TO LOOK FOR

After your play testers have finished playing the game, try asking them questions about the game to determine what worked and what didn't work. Right now, you're testing the mechanics and basics of your game, so the questions you should be asking in this chapter are radically different than ones you may ask later on in the development cycle.

Here are some examples of what to ask at this stage:

- **What was the goal of the game?** Although this may seem like an obvious question to you, it might not have been as obvious to the players. Ask if they were able to easily determine what they had to do in the game. If necessary, see if there is anything you can do to make the objectives clearer.

- **Did you experience any bugs or glitches within the game? If so, what were they?** You probably have an idea of what most of the bugs in your game are at this point, if you noticed any at all. The game is still in its early stages so the bugs should be at a minimum at this point, but you never know if some of the pickup items aren't working or if a platform may not act the way it should. Playing the game can indicate some early bugs that are easily fixed.

- **What were the controls?** This question seems obvious, but you never know what players may have struggled with early on. Sometimes players may not even know all the controls to get through a game or level. I've played games before where I didn't know about a game mechanic until I was a few levels in because there was nothing in the game to indicate its existence. If players miss a key control or even just the Sprint button, it can negatively effect their gameplay experience. Knowing if all the controls were easily understood from the early stages can help you determine if you could've given more information to the player.

- **Did you find the controls easy to learn? Why or why not?** This question goes into how long it took them to learn the controls. Keep in mind that you may know the controls off the bat, but what may seem obvious to you can be difficult to figure out for someone picking up the game for the first time. Ask how hard it was for the player to figure out the controls. Also, ask what you could do to make the process easier. The sooner players don't have to think about controls, the more fun they'll have playing the game.

- **How many times did you die in the game? What happened?** This number represents how steep a learning curve there is to your game. Because you're currently testing the first level, that number should be low. Understanding how many times and why the player died can give you information about whether your game is clear on what the player is supposed to do. If the player kept dying bumping into the enemy, maybe the enemy wasn't clearly enough depicted. If they kept falling off the edge, maybe the jump button wasn't working or wasn't clearly indicated.

- **Did the game make sense?** It's still early in the game's development, so there's probably not much to understand beyond the general mechanics of the game, but it's still important that even something as simple as what an enemy does and what a pickup item does are clear to the player.

- **What would you change at this stage?** This question is probably the trickiest of the questions because it can be affected by personal preferences. Still, it's a question I find important to ask because, while you're developing your game, there will be ideas that you just won't think of or will miss. Even something that you won't use can be invaluable in any artistic medium. It forces you to think about what the game you want to make really is. It could also give you new and interesting directions that you never thought of taking with the game.

These are questions that I have found helped me get the most out of play testing. It's often hard to give criticism to a person — especially a friend — so asking your play testers these questions may help them open up and be honest about the game. No matter what advice you do or don't take, honest feedback is never a bad thing.

HANDLING FEEDBACK

REMEMBER

Always seek feedback and suggestions — you won't improve your work unless you actively try to! It can be tempting to shield your art — keeping it hidden from the world — especially when you put so much effort into it. Your game is important because it's something you put effort into, so when someone criticizes it, that criticism can feel personal. Whenever you ask for feedback, just remember that your work can always be improved. Just because it isn't perfect doesn't mean it's bad.

Constructive feedback is always a good thing, *especially* when it's negative. There is always room for improvement on any game, and having feedback on what does or doesn't work prevents a game from falling stagnant. Asking people to play your game and give honest constructive feedback can be scary, but the sooner you overcome that fear, the better a game developer you'll be.

FINDING THE PROBLEMS IN YOUR GAME

Even the game you make in this book is not immune from critique and improvements. Games can always be improved on. This game also has its fair share of bugs and design problems that are in the game. You'll probably find problems that were missed in this chapter. Be sure to have someone test the game even beyond the problems addressed here. As an example, I've answered some of the questions listed earlier and expanded on what does and doesn't work in the game:

• **What was the goal of the game?** The game's goal isn't defined. Although there are definitely distinctive differences between the pickup items and the enemies, there is nothing to indicate what the player is supposed to accomplish in the game.

The main objective, the final pickup item in the level, has nothing beyond a simple color palette swap to indicate its importance. When designing the game's goals, there should be a larger emphasis to differentiate it from the rest of the items in the game. The goals need to be better defined from the start to give a the player direction.

- **Did you experience any bugs or glitches within the game? If so, what were they?** There is a glitch within the game that happens when the character is against the wall. When the character jumps when on a wall, the character is actually able to climb the wall because the character is reading the wall as part of the ground. This makes some of the areas in the game far less difficult than they were supposed to be.

- **What were the controls?** The controls are fairly straightforward, but the addition of the Shift key is easy to miss as you play the game, making sections of the game impossible to get through. The game needs to introduce the controls to the players. Without that, players will have a tough time figuring out all the controls of the game.

- **Did you find the controls easy to learn? Why or why not?** The controls in the game are straightforward enough that they don't really need much introduction, but there should be a guide to help the players figure out what the controls are initially. Without this guide, players may struggle to figure out the controls in the beginning. At the very least, there should be an indication about the Sprint button.

- **How many times did you die in the game? What happened?** The major problem in the game was that the first object that you can interact with can kill you, which can deter you from collecting the pickup items. Most players will die right away, not realizing that the pickup items act as health against the enemy creatures. The best solution for this would be to add another pickup item at the start of the level.

- **Did the game make sense?** The game does make sense, even if the goals are initially unclear. When the player understands the mechanics of the game and knows what items are bad and good, there is a consistency to the rest of the game.

- **What would you change at this stage?** The biggest change that needs to be made at this stage of the game is an inclusion of some guidelines that teach the player the controls of the game. The other part that should be added at this stage of the game is an ability to easily leave the game-over screen. Right now, the only way for the player to get out of a game-over is to restart the entire game, which kills flow and prevents the player from trying the game over. It's unintentionally punishing.

The camera is also locked at an angle that doesn't work the entire time. The player should be able to adjust the camera as needed, depending on what's going on in the level. Although the first level is uncomplicated and can be played without camera adjustments, any future levels that are more intricate will fall apart.

REMEMBER

Play testing is a developer's best way to determine what parts of the game work and what parts don't. You'll learn the ways to fix the problems found during play testing in Chapter 7, but the important takeaway from this chapter is how play testing can be used to help improve your final game.

A lot of these problems were left intentionally so that you can learn what types of problems a proper play test looks for. The goal is to look for problems that can break the player's immersion in the game. The worst crime a game can commit is to break the player immersion, so anything like large bugs in the code or unfavorable design choices can cause players to step out of the game and lose interest.

Fixing and Adjusting Your Game

In this chapter, you fix some of the issues in your game that I cover in Chapter 6. Not every issue will be fixed within this chapter — I cover resetting your game and camera controls in Chapter 14. Here, you adjust your level design to better introduce players to the game as well as add a very basic user interface (UI) tutorial that will change as the game needs.

This chapter also teaches you more about raycasting and using it to prevent your player from simply climbing the walls. This chapter's main goal is to go into more detail about some of the concepts discussed in previous chapters and give a quick rundown of what you've learned before continuing into animation and modeling in Chapter 8.

TURNING CRITICISM INTO CONSTRUCTION

After every play test, make a list of things that were discussed or found within the play test — good and bad. This list will allow you to see all the things in your game that are and aren't working, as well as allow you to prioritize what parts of the game are important to address now and what parts will need to be addressed later.

When you develop games, you have to prioritize problems and bugs that come up. Some problems will need to be solved earlier than others. In a world filled with deadlines, bugs that break the game need to be fixed before aesthetic problems. Think of it like homework: Some projects or assignments need to be prioritized due to the day that they're due or their importance to your overall grade. Game making is similar, except the only person who can determine the importance of certain problems over others is you! Ask yourself what problems are actually hurting the gameplay experience the most and what problems can wait for later.

In the case of this game, here are the major problems:

- **Players are punished unfairly.** This breaks the game by killing the player early on and giving the players a "game over" right in the beginning.

- **Players have issues early in the game learning the different controls.** To fix this you want to add a tutorial that will actually change as players learn the controls and demonstrate them in game.

- **Players are climbing the walls.** In a platformer, you want your players to learn how to jump and master the controls. If there are easy workarounds for the player that they can use instead, the challenging parts that make the game a game will be ineffective. And, as the game gets harder, the difficulty spike will feel uneven because the less challenging parts meant to teach the controls and parts of the game will just be ignored.

In the following sections, I walk you through solving each of these three problems.

PUNISHING YOUR PLAYER LESS

When players start the game, everything is new to them. They aren't sure what's a good thing and what's an enemy. In the early parts of the game, all players have is the information you provide them. In your game, the first major object that players interact with gives them a "game over" screen, which creates a poor association between the player and the other objects within the game, including the good ones. You can use visual clues all you want to help indicate which things are good and which things are bad, but these visual clues aren't guaranteed to work. As a general rule, the first mistakes the players make should be learning opportunities for later in the game.

The best way to fix this problem is to lessen the punishment for making the mistake. But instead of changing the code to prevent the instant death, there is a simpler way to give players a second chance after that mistake: Place a pickup right before the first enemy (see Figure 7-1).

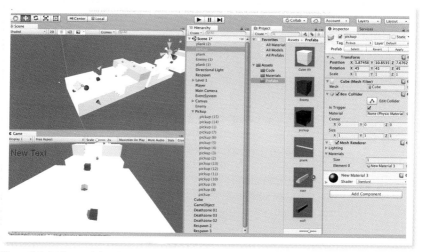

Figure 7-1: Adding a pickup item.

This may seem like a small change, but not every change in game design has to be large to make a huge difference. By adding a pickup item before the first obstacle, you're teaching two lessons with one item:

- **Players learn the benefit of the pickup items early because they see their scores increase from the start.** That way, they'll associate the two things with each other.

- **Players learn that there are beneficial items in the game from the start, giving a positive reinforcement.**

After they see this pickup item, they'll see the enemy character and one of two things will happen:

- They'll realize that the character is an enemy and avoid it.

- They'll bump into the character and lose one point.

REMEMBER

The punishment must match the mistake, or players will stop playing the game. Adding a pickup before the first enemy helps reduce the first punishment so that players learn and don't get annoyed.

The brilliance of adding just one pickup item before the enemy is that players not only learn that pickup items are good, but also learn that enemies are bad without having to restart the game. They're punished, but not too harshly. They learn what to avoid and what can be interacted with.

CREATING A USER INTERFACE TUTORIAL

Players can figure out a lot on their own, but a simple tutorial can go a long way toward preventing players from feeling frustrated. Games are only fun when you know how to play them. If you don't know how to play them, games can become more tedious than they're worth. Tutorials are a simple way to help address the problem of learning how to play.

Because the game you're working on doesn't have any really complex controls, the tutorial itself doesn't need to be very complicated — but it's still necessary. In the days of Super Mario Bros. or the arcade games, tutorials weren't necessary because there were so few controls and buttons that the player could actually use — figuring out the controls only took a minute or so. These days, games have at least ten buttons on the controllers and over a hundred on keyboards. And that doesn't include all the different combinations of controls that are now available through coding. Learning how to play a game isn't as simple for people who've never played before.

To create a UI tutorial for your game, you need to create a new UI. Follow these steps:

1. **Choose GameObject ⇨ UI ⇨ Text.**

2. **Adjust the text so that it's in the lower left of the canvas and it's a color that will stick out and can be clearly read.**

3. **Delete all the text in the text box.**

4. **From the Text (script) drop-down, there is a paragraph section. In that section you will see Horizontal Overflow with a drop-down next to it. Change it from Wrap to Overflow.**

   This prevents the text from being cut off if it's too long.

5. **Rename it "Direction Text."**

6. **Open the Char code.**

7. **At the very top of the code, enter** public Text directionText; **below where the** winText **and** countText **are.**

8. **In the** void Start () **string, enter** directionText.text = "W=Forward A=Left S=Back D=Right".

   This displays the tutorial text at the start of the game. The start of the tutorial should just give the basic controls so that players are able to see the initial controls right off the bat and get the hang of them before moving onto the next codes.

The next codes are actually going to be placed within the if statements that control the keys.

The first one will be put into the key that controls just the forward movement (W). The code shown in Figure 7-2 gives the tutorial the cue to change.

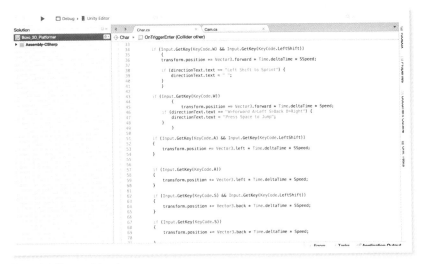

Figure 7-2: The tutorial code.

Currently, if the W key is pressed, all that happens is that the character moves forward.

1. Add an `if` statement inside of this code: `if (directionText.text == "W=Forward A=Left S=Back D=Right") {`.

   This will make it so that if you press the W key, and if the `directionText` is the starting text, the following code will happen.

2. Inside this `if` statement, add `directionText.text == "Press Space to Jump";`.

   This will change the `directionText` to the next step in the tutorial.

3. Go to the jump code (`KeyCode.Space`).

4. Follow steps 1 and 2 but change the `directionText.text` in Step 1 from `W=Forward A=Left S=Back D=Right` to `Press Space to Jump` and change the `directionText.text` in Step 2 from `Press Space to Jump` to `Left Shift to Sprint`.

5. Go to the forward sprint code (`KeyCode.W && KeyCode.LeftShift`).

6. Follow steps 1 and 2 (again) but change the `directionText.text` in Step 1 from `Press Space to Jump` to `Left Shift to Sprint` and change the `directionText.text` in Step 2 from `Left Shift to Sprint` to `" "`.

Now the players will be taken through a tutorial. When they do what the tutorial suggests, the tutorial's text will change. Save the code and exit out to Unity. Use the target next to "Direction Test" to select the object "Direction Text."

PREVENTING WALL CLIMBING WITH RAYTRACING

Raytracing works by determining whether an object is touching another object. It creates a cone in one direction that gives the player the ability to read when it's touching another object or is close to another object. You can indicate when objects are approaching or are around the object or determine if a player is a certain distance away from the ground or wall.

Before you do anything else, you need to add an extra bit of code to the jump string. As it is right now, the code will work and make sure that the character is touching the ground when the character is jumping. At the end of the `if` statement, add `&& Groundtouch == True`. This way, the code will know that the only time the player can jump is when the player presses the Spacebar and is touching the ground.

Now, before you can add the wall touching code, you need to add a new bool at the top of the code. `public bool wc = false` is similar to the `gc` code. That's because all you're doing is using the `gc` code as a reference point for the `wc` code.

Right under the `Vector3` for `gc`, add a new `Vector3` that is the exact same as the `gc` code but instead of down, the direction is `Vector3 . Forward`. That way, the player will be using the raytrace forward and will be able to tell that there is an object right in front of it. The difference between the codes comes in the result of the code. The `gc` code was created to determine if the player is touching the ground or not, and the `wc` code prevents players from climbing the walls.

The easiest solution to this problem is to prevent the character from being able to move forward past the wall. Like the enemy code before, this can be accomplished by moving the character a distance back every time the player touches the object from the front. At the top of the code, add a new float for the code. Add to the top of the wall `public float wall = 20f`. This will prevent the character from being able to progress through the level without jumping over the gaps. The number 20 works because it's faster backward than the sprint is forward so there is no way to use the sprint with the jump bottom to just undercut the parts of the game with jumping.

The raytracing needs a complete number for it to work. **Right now, the code as listed as .5. You need to change that to 0.5. Otherwise, computers won't recognize the number as a decimal and assume it's just 5.**

Underneath the `Vector3 gc` code, place the `wc` code shown in Figure 7-3. Then create an `if` statement underneath it: `if (Physics.Raycast (transform.position, wc. 0.5f))`. This determines when there is an object in front of the character. When there is, the character will move backward by the wall distance defined earlier. This code will prevent the character from climbing the wall, but it will also create a problem with how your character interacts with the enemy characters. For this, I find 0.4f actually works better than 0.5f because it gives just enough distance so that the walls are still causing the character to move back and prevents climbing, but it also keeps the enemy characters from bouncing right off of you.

Figure 7-3: The wall touch code.

Save this code and go back into Unity. While in Unity, select any one of the enemy characters. Go into the Inspector window and go down to the box collider. Change the collider's size to (0.5,0.5,0.5,). Now the character will be unable to simply climb the walls and still be affected by the enemy characters.

CHAPTER

08

Animating in Blender

Unity is excellent game-developing software, but it's limited in its ability to actually create characters or environments for your game. In this chapter, you'll learn about another program that you can use to help bring life to your game: Blender. This chapter will help you learn the basics of Blender so that you can model and animate your characters and obstacles within your game.

Blender can be intimidating when you first open it. This chapter helps you navigate the interface without getting lost in all the things that Blender is able to do. In this chapter, you'll create and edit a single object, as well as learn about the different parts of a 3D mesh and how you can use them to bring your characters to life.

MIXING THINGS UP WITH BLENDER

Blender is a open-source 3D animation creation suite. What that means is that it's a program with multiple uses in 3D development. Modeling, rigging, animation, motion tracking, and even editing and game development are all things that Blender can be used to work on. It does this through community-driven updates. Users are not only able to but are encouraged to work on and change the code that Blender runs off of. This has led to a strong community within Blender that has been crucial to Blender being the versatile and free program that it is today.

For your game, you'll mostly be using Blender's modeling and animation capabilities to help craft the characters and obstacles that will be within your game. Creating assets is a key part of developing your game, because this is the part of game design that is about bringing to life the original vision for your game. This is not an animation book, nor is it a book about Blender. But by learning the basics of Blender and how to bring files and models you created from Blender into your game, you'll be able to customize and personalize your game in ways you wouldn't be able to simply within Unity.

DOWNLOADING BLENDER

Before you can use Blender you have to download it. Luckily Blender is available to everyone for free across all computer platforms — Windows, Mac, and Linux.

1. Go to **www.blender.org (see Figure 8-1).**

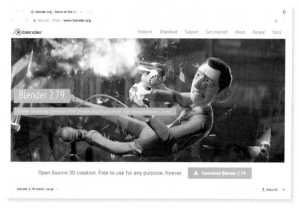

Figure 8-1: Blender's website.

2. **At the top of the page, click Download.**

   Blender will automatically determine what type of platform you're using (Windows, Mac, or Linux).

3. **Click Download Blender.**

   The file will download.

4. **Move the file into the applications folder on your computer.**

OPENING BLENDER FOR THE FIRST TIME

When you open Blender the first time, you'll see the screen shown in Figure 8-2. Here, you'll see the version number of Blender that you downloaded, along with some links to other things about Blender, including a place to donate to Blender and a link to the website. You'll also see a Recent section, which will be empty because you haven't created a project yet. To get rid of this screen overlay, click to the side of it; you'll be brought to the base Blender interface.

Part of the appeal of Blender is its customizability. You can change the interface to match your style of working, but for the purposes of this book, I suggest sticking to the base interface.

In the center of the window is the 3D View. This is similar to the Scene view in Unity. It's where the majority of your work will be focused. In the 3D View, you'll notice a grid with a box in the center. This grid shows the x-, y-, and z-axes. The first major difference you'll notice between Unity and Blender is the fact that the y- and z-axes are swapped with each other, with the *y*-axis going along the grid and the *z*-axis going toward and away from the grid. Unity will automatically adjust for this when importing the files from Blender into Unity so it won't cause an issue, but it is something you'll want to keep in mind when creating your characters and animations.

3D View   Information Window   3D Outliner

Timeline   Properties Editor

Figure 8-2: Blender's opening screen.

On the top of the screen, you'll notice the Information window. This is where the majority of the configuration settings are located. You can also save using this section.

At the bottom of the screen, you'll see the Timeline. This controls the animations that you'll be making, giving you the ability to insert keyframes and adjust your animation along the frame count.

In the upper-right corner of the screen, you'll see the 3D Outliner. This shows you all the objects that are in the scene. Underneath the outliner, you'll see the Properties Editor. This is where you can adjust the properties of the scene or object, change the material, or even add modifiers or constraints to an object.

CREATING A NEW FILE IN BLENDER

To create a new file in Blender, choose File⟶New. When a popup appears, click Reload Start-Up File.

Whenever you create a new file, the scene will reset to include just a cube, a camera, and a light. This is the standard setup in Blender. To delete an object such as a camera, light, or cube in the scene, simply select the item you want to delete and press X on your keyboard. A popup will appear asking if you're sure that you want to delete this object. Click yes or simply press X again. The object will then be deleted.

When you're creating your characters or objects for your game, you'll want to delete the camera and the light because you don't want them to be transferred over to Unity, which already has a light and camera in the scene.

FIGURING OUT THE BLENDER INTERFACE

Blender is a great program for animation and modeling, but like Unity, it's intimidating to open the first time. In the following section, I introduce you to the different parts of Blender's interface and explain how to properly use the program. Knowing the layout of Blender will be invaluable when using this program to help build the characters and objects for your game.

TABS

On the left side of the 3D View section, there is a menu. On the far left of the menu, there are multiple tabs that you can select. The tabs differ depending on what mode you're in.

The only two tabs that you need to worry about in Chapters 9 and 10 are the Create and Tools tabs.

TOOLS TAB

The Tools tab (see Figure 8-3) alters the selected object.

When you're in Object mode, this involves the transformation controls, mirroring, deleting, changing the origin, and the type of shading.

When you're in Edit Mode, the Tools tab opens up different options for editing your object, from extruding to deleting faces.

Figure 8-3: The Tools tab.

CREATE TAB

The Create tab (see Figure 8-4) allows you to create different objects within the scene, from a square to a sphere. It also allows you to create paths, cameras, and even light sources for the scene.

When you create an object in Object mode, both objects are the same unless you combine or join them together later.

Do not use create in Edit Mode unless you absolutely need to.

Figure 8-4: Create tab.

RELATIONS TAB

The Relations tab shows you the various grouping options you have for an object. It can parent objects to one another, create group of objects, or link objects together.

ANIMATION TAB

The Animation tab gives you the ability to create and delete keyframes in the animation, as well as bake certain motions (create all the individual frames in a sequence as opposed to the computer just inferring that motion).

PHYSICS TAB

The Physics tab allows you to adjust the mass of an object and apply physics with a rigid body similar to how Unity does it.

GREASE PENCIL TAB

The Grease Pencil tab is a way to add annotations and animation notes into the scene that you can use as reference points. Grease pencils can also be used to assist in 2D animation within Unity.

SHADING AND UV TAB

The shading and UV tab gives you the ability to modify the way the object is rendered (whether its lines are hard or smooth in the render), as well as how to fix or adjust faces on the object that may be inversed.

UV mapping is also available to help texture the character or object by creating or marking "seams."

OPTION TAB

This is the mesh option menu, which gives you control over the X-mirror and Edge Select mode. The X-mirror tools allow you to edit your object symmetrically. If you make a change on one side of the object, that change will happen on the other side along the x-axis. The Edge Select mode gives you the ability to adjust the edge's path, giving it a curve or bevel.

THE OUTLINER

On the upper right of the screen, you'll see the Outliner for the project (see Figure 8-5). The Outliner serves three purposes:

- It allows you to select different objects without needing to locate them within the scene.

- It allows you to parent objects to each other by simply dragging the object you want to parent into its parent.

Figure 8-5: The Outliner.

- It allows you to adjust which objects can be viewed, selected, or rendered.

- The eyeball next to the object determines if the object can be seen in the scene. Selecting it will turn the object invisible in the scene, but the object will still be rendered if you render the scene.

- Clicking the cursor will stop the object from being able to be selected in the scene, locking it from being changed beyond any changes that have already been made to it within the scene.

- The camera determines what objects are rendered when you render the animation. If you select the camera, it will still be seen within the scene but not within the final render.

Clicking the plus sign to the left of the object will show all the different objects linked or parented to the object. Think of all the objects in the scene as automatically coming with an external empty that they're parented to because, within this list, you'll find the mesh. Inside the mesh will be linked the material the object is using, and inside the material will be the texture the material uses.

TIMELINE

The Timeline (shown in Figure 8-6) is located at the bottom of the screen and is primarily used to control the animation within the scene. Adjusting the Timeline will adjust where the time is within the animation.

Figure 8-6: The Timeline.

You'll notice at the bottom of the Timeline that there are numbers. These numbers do *not* stand for seconds within the animation — they stand for frames. In animation frames are the pictures that fly by at a fraction of a second to create the illusion of movement. There are different frame rates for different media, but the three that you should know are as follows:

- **24 frames per second (FPS):** Standard film

- **30 FPS:** Minimum game standard

- **60 FPS:** High definition

For your game, you'll be going off of 30 FPS. The numbers at the bottom of the screen will indicate what frame you're on, as well as the start and end frames for the animation.

Also on the Timeline you'll find a control panel that will allow you to play, rewind, fast-forward, or pause your animation. You'll also see a red button, which turns on *automatic keyframing,* so whenever you move or adjust your object in the scene, Blender will automatically record a keyframe to mark the position change. If you move along the Timeline and then move the object, Blender will make another keyframe instead of overwriting, causing your object or character to move. You can also turn off automatic keyframing by simply clicking the autokeyframing button again.

PROPERTIES SECTION

Similar to the Create and Tools tabs, the Properties section of the window has different tabs for the objects. The first four tabs are for the properties not relating directly to the object:

- **Camera:** Render settings. Render settings are how you can export an animation. Think of these as setting up a camera to shoot a part of a movie. The render settings translate the animations and 3D objects into pictures/movies that can be watched.

  In the render settings, you can set the following (and more):

  - **Resolution:** How detailed the animation is.

  - **Frame count:** The amount of frames (pictures) per second there are in animation. Thirty frames per second is the average for games.

  - **Output location:** Where the final animation/picture will be saved to on the computer.

- **Pictures:** Render layer settings. The render layers show what layers in the animation are visible when rendered. It is possible to layer your animation like a Photoshop file or collage and make different layers visible at any moment.

- **Light, Sphere, and Cylinder:** The scene settings. In the scene settings, you can adjust the settings of the scene itself, including choosing a main camera to render the animation out of and adjusting the scene to include audio or even add gravity and rigidbody settings to the scene.

- **World:** The environmental/background settings. These settings control the color of the background when the scene is rendered, giving you control over the horizon and the natural lighting within the scene.

- **Cube:** The object settings. These settings control the transformation controls, display options, and group settings of the object. In this tab, you can move the object around the scene, place it in different layers in the scene, and group the object with other objects for importing and exporting purposes.

Blender has a ton of redundant controls within it. There are usually multiple ways to do the same thing. The object settings are just one example of this — all the tools available in it are able to be done in different parts of Blender. Keep that in mind when looking through Blender.

- **Chain:** Constraint controls. These controls allow you to link objects together. Unlike the group controls, which do not alter the objects, the constraint controls will directly affect how the object moves in the scene. Objects that are parented to other objects move when those objects are moved. The constraint controls give you a variety of ways to link two objects together in a scene within the drop-down.

- **Wrench:** Modifier controls. The modifier controls can alter the shape, size, or even smoothness of the objects. In the modifier controls, you can select from the drop-down a number of different modifiers that can alter your object.

- **Upside-down triangle:** Object data. The object data of an object contains the texture space, vertex groups, and shape keys for an object. This is a breakdown of different changes to the data of an object. As an example, the shape keys in this menu can be used to alter the shape of the object to different key positions.

- **Sphere:** Material settings. The materials are the colors and look of your object. In here, you can change those visual settings to give your object different colors, transparencies, and even reflections.

- **Checkerboard:** The texture settings. Textures are like pictures or patterns that you put on top of a material. The texture settings give you the ability to add pictures or bump maps to your object to help give the object more life and dimension.

- **Stars:** The particle effect controller. Gives you the option of adding particle effects to your animations, such as rain or explosions. These settings can also be used to create other things such as hair or grass on your object.

- **Ball Bouncing:** The physics control on the object. This controls all the physics settings on the object. These can include the rigidbody settings on a specific object or even fluid simulations.

NAVIGATING THE INTERFACE

This section explains how to navigate a 3D space within Blender. The navigation settings are similar to the ones you use in Unity, but it's still important to understand the differences between the programs. In order to properly use Blender, you must be comfortable navigating a 3D space within the program.

PANNING, ROTATING, AND ZOOMING

As with Unity, your best friends in a 3D space are your navigation tools. The Panning, Rotating, and Zooming tools in Blender are similar to those in Unity, but there some differences in how these tools work in Blender:

- **Panning:** To pan on the screen, click and hold the middle mouse button while also holding down the Shift key and moving the mouse.

- **Rotating:** To rotate around the scene, hold down the middle mouse button and move the mouse.

- **Zooming:** To Zoom in and out of the scene, roll the middle mouse button in and out. Rolling the middle mouse button toward you zooms the camera toward the scene. Rolling the middle mouse button away from you zooms the camera out of the scene.

When you're working with Blender, you should use a mouse, not a track-pad. Blender's interface wasn't designed for trackpads. There are ways to adjust the settings to use a trackpad, but it's not as well developed as the mouse.

TRANSFORMATION TOOLS

The transformation tools adjust the position, rotation, and scale of the selected object. In Edit Mode, these tools can also be used to transform the vertices, edges, or faces of an object.

At the bottom of the Scene window and above the Timeline, you'll see three different blue buttons next to a Global drop-down. These are the transformation tools:

- **Global/Local**: The Global drop-down shows the different axes that the object can be adjusted along. The only two you need to know are the global and local axes. The global axis aligns with the world's axis and will never change. The local axis changes along the axis of the object.

- **Translation tool (see Figure 8-7)**: The button with the arrow pointing up is the Translation tool. Selecting this button will show three arrows along the axis (global or local) that you can choose to move the object along.

REMEMBER

Green is the *y*-axis, blue is the *z*-axis, and red is the *x*-axis.

The Translation tool changes the position of the object. Another way to access this tool is to press G (for grab) on your keyboard. This will pick up the object so that you can move it along the 3D space, but if you want to move it along a certain axis, just select the axis you want to move it along (X, Y, or Z) and press the corresponding key on the keyboard (the X key for the *x*-axis, the Y key for the *y*-axis, and the Z key for the *z*-axis). Doing so will lock to the object on that axis.

You can also right-click the box to pick it up and move it to a different position, but you must left-click to place the object. If you right-click again, the object will reset back to its origin.

- **Rotation tool (Figure 8-8)**: The curved-line button is the Rotation tool. When you click it, your object will be surrounded by three different lines for rotating around a particular axis. The white circle will rotate along the view's axis.

The Rotation tool changes the rotation of the object. You can also rotate the object by pressing R (for rotate) on your keyboard. This will rotate the object along the view's axis, but by pressing the button on the keyboard that corresponds with the axis, you want the object will rotate around those particular axes.

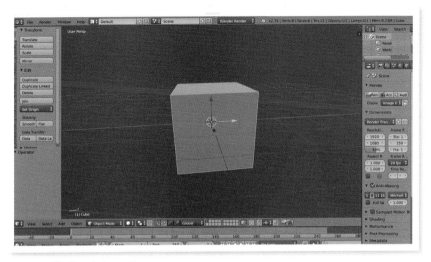

Figure 8-7: The Translation tool.

- **Scale tool (see Figure 8-9):** The button marked with a line with a square at the end is the Scale tool. Clicking this button will show lines along the axes with cubes around them. Clicking and dragging these cubes will scale along that particular axis from the origin point of the object.

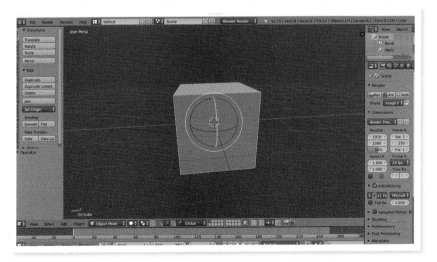

Figure 8-8: The Rotation tool.

The Scale tool changes the size of the object. You can also scale the object by pressing S on your keyboard. This will scale the box uniformly (all at once), but by pressing the button on the keyboard that corresponds with the axis you want, the object will scale along that same axis.

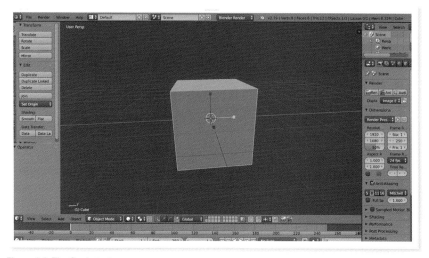

Figure 8-9: The Scale tool.

EDITING YOUR OBJECT

You use Blender to create the assets for your videogame because you can create complex shapes within Blender. You can alter the shape of your objects by switching to Edit Mode (see Figure 8-10). You can switch to Edit Mode in two ways.

The first way to switch to Edit Mode is to go down above the Timeline where it says Object Mode and select from the Edit Mode drop-down menu.

The other way to get to Edit Mode is by pressing the Tab key on your keyboard. This will switch to Edit Mode from whatever mode you're in. If you're already in Edit Mode, pressing Tab will switch your mode back to the last mode you were in before Edit Mode.

There are several other modes that Blender has that you won't be using but should know about:

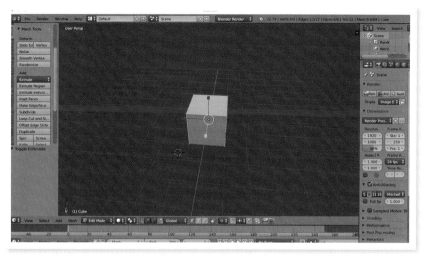

Figure 8-10: Edit Mode.

- **Object Mode:** Allows you to move objects around and animate your character.

- **Sculpt Mode:** Gives you the ability to sculpt the shape of the object as if it were like clay. (It requires many vertices to use.)

- **Weight Paint:** Helps you rig your characters to a skeletal structure. This is useful for creating characters that move and emote.

- **Texture Paint:** Paints textures onto the object.

- **Vertex Paint:** Similar to Texture Paint but paints the vertices directly.

VERTICES, EDGES, AND FACES

When you enter Edit Mode, you're changing the *mesh* (shape) of the object. There are three parts that make up a mesh: the vertices, the edges, and the faces. You can change the mesh by altering the position, rotation, size, or number of vertices, edges, or faces. Next to where you found the transformation tools, you'll see three new orange buttons:

- **Vertex Select tool:** The small orange dot at the edge of a cube button is the Vertex Select tool. *Vertices* (shown in Figure 8-11) are the points of any object. They mark the points on the object where an edge ends. Vertices are the smallest part of an object.

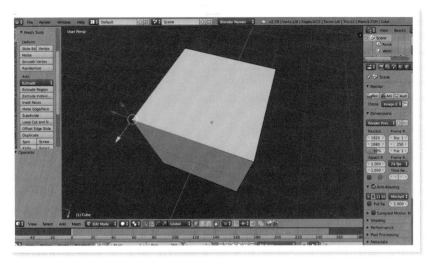

Figure 8-11: Vertices.

- **Edge Select tool:** The orange line on the cube button is the Edge Select tool. Edges (shown in Figure 8-12) are the lines between two vertices. They mark the lines on the object and are used to make up a face.

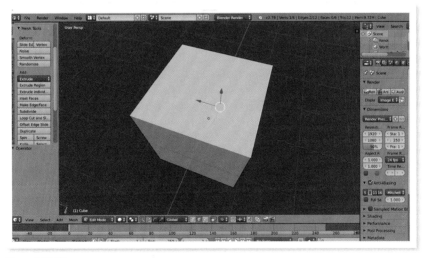

Figure 8-12: Edges.

- **Face Select tool:** The orange square on the front of the cube button is the Face Select tool. Faces (shown in Figure 8-13) are made up of at *least* three edges and make up the visual part of an object. Whenever you see an object, you're seeing the faces of the object as they wrap around to make the mesh.

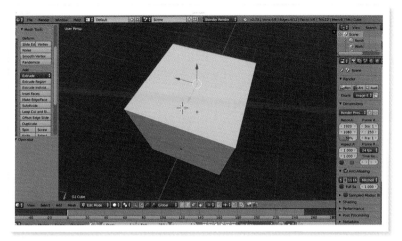

Figure 8-13: Faces.

TIP

Whenever you create a new object, you want all the faces to be quads (four sides) if possible. If the mesh ever has to be deformed or changed, quads are able to do so easier than faces with three or five or more sides. Quads are your best friend.

EDITING TOOLS

There are a ton of different options when it comes to the tools you can use to edit your object. On the Tools tab, you have at the least 34 different tools you can use to change your object, and that's not counting the different variations some of the tools offer. For now, you only need to really know four of these tools:

- **Loop-Cut Slide (Ctrl+R):** The Loop-Cut Slide tool (shown in Figure 8-14) creates a new edge that wraps around the object. This creates new edges and vertices that can be edited and cuts the faces in two. When you use the Loop-Cut Slide tool, select one of the edges that you want your line to go around. It will appear as a pink line wrapping around the edge. When you have the edge you want, left-click it. This will change the line to a yellow line, but it hasn't been placed yet. After you clicked the first time, the line can now be adjusted along the edge selected. When the new edge is where you want it to be, simply left-click again to place the edge loop.

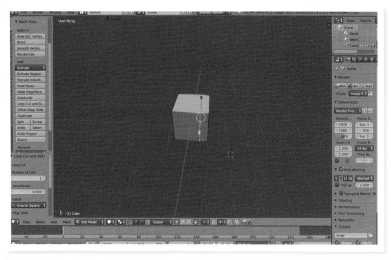

Figure 8-14: Loop-Cut Slide tool.

- **Extrude (E):** The Extrude tool (shown in Figure 8-15) helps you build out from a face or edge (vertices, too, but these don't work as well). The Extrude tool expands the selected face or edge out and creates new edges or faces to keep the face connected to the overall mesh. This tool allows you to build out and customize an object from the different faces or edges. When you use the Extrude tool, it will extrude the face toward or away from the mesh (you can extrude inward as well). Left clicking after you extrude will place the extrusion, which you can then adjust the size and position of.

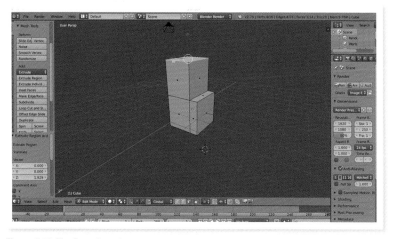

Figure 8-15: The Extrude tool.

- **Inset Face (I):** The Inset face tool (see Figure 8-16) creates a face within the selected face(s). This face will shrink in from the edges and have edges connecting its vertices to the vertices of the face that's being inset. This tool can be used to create smaller faces within the different faces to create objects such as staircases or windows. When you use the Inset Face tool, be sure not to shrink the Face tool too much to cross the vertices. The tool should create quads along its edges. Left-click to confirm the inset face.

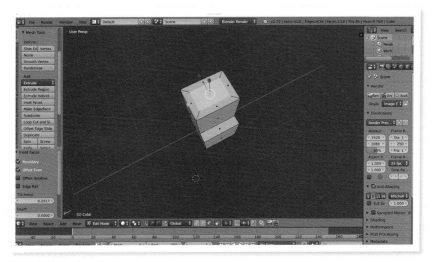

Figure 8-16: The Inset Face tool.

Do not cross vertices! Crossing vertices occurs when edges or faces intersect with each other and cross each other. The computer will not read these faces properly, and the mesh will not work properly if the vertices are crossed. Always count your vertices and prevent them from crossing.

- **Insert Face (F):** The Insert Face tool creates a face in between two edges if no face exists. As an example of this, delete one of the faces on your mesh. Select the face and press X. When you're asked if you want to delete the face, confirm that you do. Now switch to Edge Select Mode and select two edges that are opposite of each other (hold Shift to select multiple edges or faces at once). Click the Insert Face tool, and a new face will appear in its place. Connect to both edges as well as any other edges connected to those vertices. This can be useful because the inside of the face doesn't render properly. Only the exterior of a face renders properly so to create doorways, you'll have to create and combine faces.

- **Creating your own:** After you test out the different tools discussed here, switch back to Object Mode and delete the object by pressing X. Go to the Create tab and create a new object and place it on the grid. Use the Inset Face, Extrude, Loop-Cut Slide, and Insert Face tool to create your own object — a fancy water fountain, an Aztec temple (see Figure 8-17), or something else of your own creation. In Chapter 9, you'll create assets for the game, but before you do so, make sure that you have a firm grasp on how Blender works by creating some objects of your own.

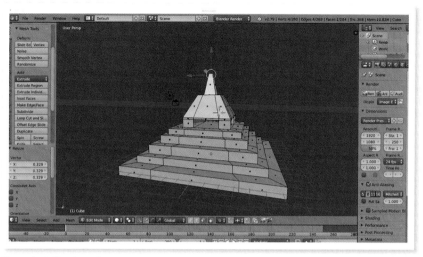

Figure 8-17: The Aztec Temple.

CHAPTER

09

Creating Your Assets

You've designed your first level and played around with Blender. In this chapter, you'll learn how to bring your game to life. Up until this point in the book, you've been seeing how to make your game playable and how to create your basic game mechanics and code. You've created the skeleton and muscle of your game. Now it's time to give it its skin.

In this chapter, you'll learn how to not only design and create your characters, but also add a material to your characters within Blender. I explain how parenting works so you can link the different parts of your character together. Finally, you learn how and where you should save your project to utilize Unity and Blender to their fullest.

THINKING ABOUT THEME AND STYLE

Before you begin to create your characters for your game, you need to think about the theme and style discussed in Chapter 1. Think about how different a game would be if instead of a plumber hopping on mushrooms, it was an alien hopping on astronauts. The mechanics and goals may be the same, but the different theme and style change the feel of the game. The mechanics are the most important part of any game, but the theme is what introduces players to the world and pushes them to actually play the game.

Theme helps give your game a story and a purpose. The mechanics may have an objective, but the theme gives a player a goal. You aren't just getting to the end of a level — you're defeating a dragon. When you make your game, you have to consider what you want your players to feel when they play it.

THEME: THE LANGUAGE OF YOUR GAME

The theme of the game is the story. Who your characters *are* matters just as much as what they're doing. Before you build your characters, ask yourself who the player is. A blue hedgehog who runs while fighting an evil egg-shaped professor with his super speed may seem like an absurd concept, but it has persisted for more than 25 years because the theme is memorable. Would Sonic have been as successful if he were anything other than a hedgehog? The theme of the game is usually the first thing people think about when they think of the game.

Mortal Kombat and Street Fighter are essentially the same type of game but for different audiences, especially when the games first came out and their controls were similar. The difference is how the games are portrayed. Street Fighter has extremely stylized characters with large muscles or petite forms fighting with large movements. Mortal Kombat goes for a more "realistic" and gruesome approach. Both games are about fighting, but they have very different themes.

Think about what you want your game to be about when you design your player and the enemies. Is the player even the "hero" of the game? Thinking about your player's place in the world of the game changes the game entirely. Even in the platformer that you're designing in this book, there are multiple options that can change what the game is about. Perhaps the player is playing as an escaped alien trying to sneak off of a space station to wreck havoc on the world below. Maybe the player is playing as a mouse trying to avoid the different traps and animals that want to stop him from getting his block of cheese. Or maybe the character is just an average person trying to avoid the creatures of the apocalypse while she tries to retrieve medical supplies for her dying daughter. Each of those game themes can fit within the game you designed but would create a completely different experience for the player. The characters, obstacles, and objectives you create matter because they tell the player what your game is about — not just what happens in the game, but what it means. A game about war can change drastically simply by changing what side you're on.

STYLE: THE ACCENT OF YOUR GAME

When you think of your game, you probably consider the mechanics or characters in the game. You may think of the theme of the game or the story, but one thing that some early developers overlook is the style of the game. Style is how your game looks. A game with the same story and characters can vary in extreme ways in just style alone, and that also changes how people perceive and play the game.

Games like Call of Duty or Modern Warfare take a more realistic approach, dulling the color palette and using more realistic proportions. On the other hand, Overwatch and Team Fortress go for a more animated and stylized approach, choosing bright colors and distinctive shapes to create their characters; large characters are larger than life, and small characters are tiny. Think about how these two approaches change how you perceive the game, as well as the audience that is attracted to the games.

The best comparison to style in media is in animation. Animated movies are all stylized in some way to attract a certain feeling or audience. Disney movies and shows use softer, more polished shapes with crisp lines that separate them from the background. This approach emphasizes the feeling of control and polish that Disney is known for in its films. Disney movies and shows are all put together with thought and care, and aim for a family audience.

Cartoon Network, on the other hand, uses a much more robust color palette and has less polished lines. Its shows aim to bring life to every part of the scene, even causing some of the characters to bleed into the background. The shows on Cartoon Network appear to swap polish for passion. Each line feels alive in the show, even if the line is dirty itself.

REMEMBER

Style changes games just as much as mechanics and story do. When you work to make your game, think about what kind of style you want in the game. Is your game going to be cartoony or realistic? Are you characters lifelike or elongated? When your characters move, how fluid or stiff are they? Before you make your assets, you should have an idea of what your the game will look like.

Tim Burton's films are all stylized to have a very dull color palette with splashes of crisp color and elongated shapes. His movies are distorted and gothic to engross audiences in his vision of the world.

Sony Animation tries to build expressive characters and focuses on 3D characters that feel like they could be 2D characters. Characters move in ways that are larger than life and more expressive than normal humans.

You'll learn more about animation and what goes into bringing the characters to life in Chapter 10, but for now just keep in mind that style changes the story even if the plot and characters don't change at all. None of the styles I just described is bad, but they do change the way you think of the films that the styles are used in. Imagine if Tim Burton did a film about an overprotective vampire trying to care for his daughter, or if Cartoon Network did a show about a talking duck and his three nephews traveling the world on adventures in search of riches.

CREATING YOUR FIRST CHARACTER

For the game you're working on in this book, the theme and style have been premade to maximize how much you'll be able to do and learn. The game is about a simple box person who is trying to escape from a robot dystopian society. The characters themselves are very cartoony in their style and will have big eyes as their key feature. This style is easy to model and animate, so you'll be able to easily build and animate your game with limited modeling and animation experience.

The main character is a blue box with two round eyes. To start making the character, open a new file in Blender. The cube that you have when you open Blender is a good place to start because it's the exact size and proportions that you'll need for your character.

CREATING THE EYES

After you open Blender and have a cube on the grid (see Figure 9-1), it's time to make the eyes for the character. The character's eyes are just simple spheres that will be in the cube. To create the eyes, follow these steps:

1. **Click the Create tab.**

2. **Scroll down to the Sphere, and rotate it 90 degrees on the _y_-axis.**

   This way, the eyes are facing forward.

3. **Scale the eye down to be smaller than the cube.**

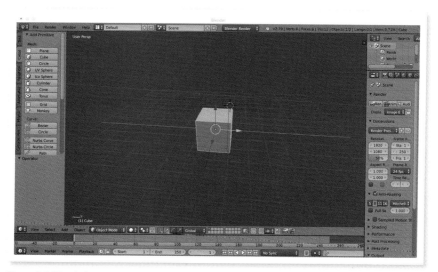

Figure 9-1: Blender's open screen.

4. **Place the eyeball in the cube so that it's sticking out of the cube as if it were an eyeball.**

5. **With the eye still selected, press Shift + D.**

   This will duplicate the eye so that there are two of them.

6. **Move the other eye to the other half of the cube so that the character has two eyes (see Figure 9-2).**

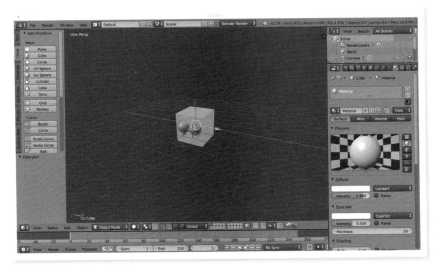

Figure 9-2: The cube with eyes.

PARENTING THE EYES TO THE BODY

After you finish making the eyes, there is still a problem in the character. The eyes don't move with the body when you move the body. Most people have no desire to leave their eyes behind when they start walking, so the best way to solve this problem is to parent the eyes to the cube. To do this, go to your outliner and find the cube and spheres.

Double-clicking the object in the outliner will give you the option to rename the objects. Rename the cube Player so that you'll be able to keep track of what object is what when you transfer everything over to Blender.

To parent the spheres to the cube, simply drag the spheres to the cube. When you do so, a little text box will pop up and say Drop to Set Parent. When you see that text box, drop the spheres and they'll be parented to the object (see Figure 9-3).

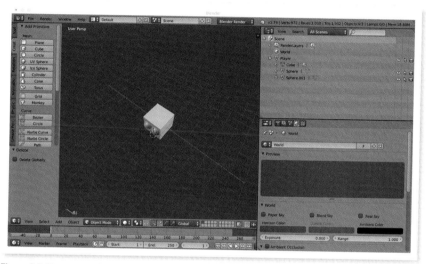

Figure 9-3: The parented eyes.

CREATING A MATERIAL FOR THE CHARACTER

After you make the eyes, it's time to add some color to your characters. You can do this in both Unity and Blender, but Blender gives you a few more options when you're making the materials for your characters.

First, make sure that you select the object you want to assign this material to. You'll be able to use the same materials for different objects later, but for now you need to create a new material because this is the first material you'll be making in the game.

To create a new material, follow these steps:

1. **Click the Material tab in the Properties section.**

2. **If no material is available, click the plus sign (+) to the right of the material box. If there is a material, skip to Step 4.**

REMEMBER

You're creating a material, not a texture, for your character. Materials act as the base that textures can be added to in Blender, but because you're creating simple characters, you don't need to worry about adding textures — materials will do just fine.

After you press the plus sign (+), you'll see that a new empty material has been made.

3. **Fill in this new empty material by clicking the New button below the material window.**

   This will create a basic Lambert material.

   Below the Preview drop-down, you'll see Diffuse and Specular. Diffuse is the color of the object; Specular is the shine of your object.

4. **Next to Diffuse, you'll see a drop-down menu. Clicking this drop-down menu will show all the different types of materials. Right now just stick with Lambert as a material, but keep in mind that each of the different materials renders slightly differently and can create different effects. The intensity is just how rich the color is.**

5. **Change the Specular color so that the object's shine isn't just white.**

   Try changing it to a light blue color to match the character's coloring.

   You can also change the *intensity* (how shiny the object is) and the *hardness* (how soft the edges of the shine are — the higher the hardness, the sharper the edges). CookTorr is similar to Lambert because there is also a drop-down menu with different options. CookTorr is just a specific type of shininess that changes the consistency of the shine on the object.

6. **Change the Diffuse color to a light blue (see Figure 9-4) and keep the Specular the same.**

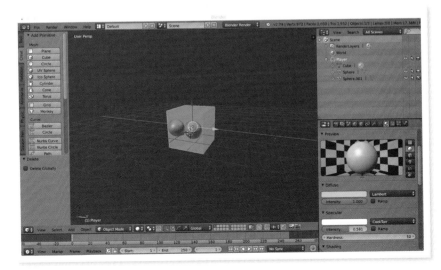

Figure 9-4: The applied material.

CREATING THE EYE MATERIALS

The materials for the eyes are done slightly differently than the body because the eyes need two different colors for the eyeball and the pupil. (You can also use these steps to create an iris, but that just involves an extra step and isn't necessary to make a decent cartoon eyeball.)

First, make sure you have either eye selected. Then follow steps 1 through 5 in the preceding section to create a white material instead of a blue one. Then follow these steps:

1. **Switch to Edit Mode.**

2. **Select the front two circles of faces (see Figure 9-5).**

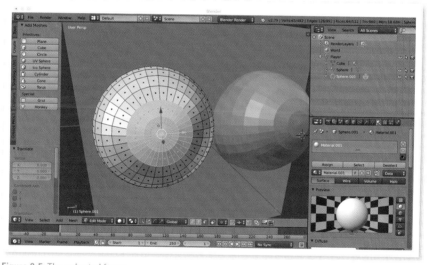

Figure 9-5: The selected faces.

You can select four-sided faces that are connected all around the mesh by holding down the Alt key and selecting the edge that they connect to the other faces on. This won't work for any faces that have more than four sides or less than four sides, but it can save you some valuable time.

3. **Click the Materials tab.**

4. **Create a new material (steps 2 and 3 in the preceding list).**

5. **Change the diffuse color to black.**

6. **Click Assign near the top.**

   This will assign the material to only the faces selected.

7. **Return to Object Mode and repeat this process for the other eye.**

To save time instead of creating whole new materials for the other eye, you can reuse the same materials. When you create a new empty material (Step 2 in creating a new material), instead of clicking New, click the material drop-down right next to it. The drop-down will list all the materials that have been made in this project. Simply click the material that matches the one that you want.

SAVING YOUR CHARACTER

After you finish creating your character (see Figure 9-6), you need to save the character so that you can use it in your game (or so that you can animate the character in Chapter 10). Before you save your character, select the lamp and camera in the scene and delete them — they won't be needed. Before you save any of the characters or objects in this game, you'll want to delete the lamp and camera.

1. **Choose File ⇨ Save As.**

2. **Locate your game folder that contains the Unity and Blender folders.**

3. **Select the Blender folder.**

4. **Change the name of the file (currently untitled.blend in Figure 9-7) to player.blend.**

5. **Click Save as Blender File.**

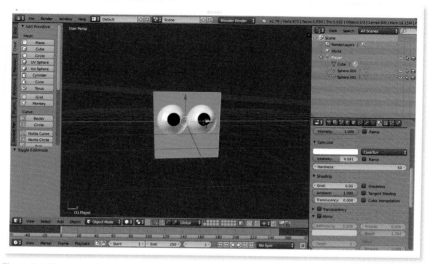

Figure 9-6: The completed character.

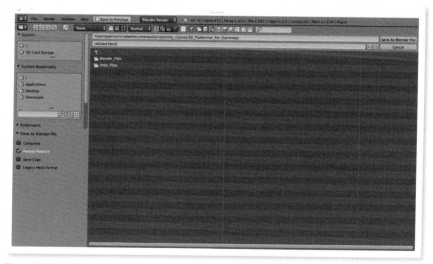

Figure 9-7: The Save screen.

This will save the project as a Blender file in the folder that you created earlier. Now you'll be able to keep your character file close to your Unity files if you ever have to transfer the files.

CREATING THE ENEMY GRUNT

The enemy grunt characters help fill your game with peril. These characters must look threatening to indicate the danger they face to the player. Generally speaking, the best way to create a threatening character is make it look mean or unfeeling. In Mario, the Goombas have eyebrows that point downward to make them look angry. In Sonic, the enemies are machines that are clearly different from the animal character that you're playing. The early Sonic villains are also insectoid to help highlight the difference. When you're designing your enemy characters, you want to also make sure that because they're grunts they don't have too many unique features and can be used interchangeably so that the player can recognize them as enemies throughout the games.

The other common thing about enemy units in platformers is that they generally move back and forth in a pattern or toward the player character to indicate hostility. I'll cover this in more detail in Chapter 10 when you learn more about animation, but for now just keep in mind that these characters should look hostile and evil.

Using your character, first delete the eyes and save the file as enemy. blend in the same location that you saved the player character file in. Then create a cylinder. This will act as the "eye" for your evil robot character that will be the enemy in the game.

1. Rotate the cylinder 90 degrees on the Y so that the top of the cylinder is facing the front.

2. Switch to Edit Mode.

3. Change the size of the back face so that it's slightly smaller than the front base (see Figure 9-8).

4. Switch to Object Mode, and move the eye into the cube so that the two objects are overlapping.

5. Switch back into Edit Mode and, using the Inset Face, Extrude, and Loop-Cut slide tools, create a lens for the eyestalk.

6. Inset the face in the front, size it down, and pull it into the cylinder slightly.

7. Extrude that face and pull it out.

8. Inset the face again two more times, each time bringing the face out slightly to create a rounder curve to the lens.

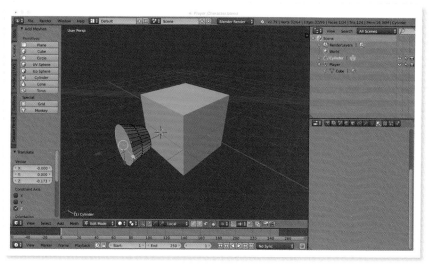

Figure 9-8: The robot's eye.

9. Loop-cut slide the side of the cylinder near the front of the cylinder.

10. Use alt-select to select all the quads around the cylinder that are near the front.

11. Using the S key as a shortcut, scale uniformly so that you create a nice expansion in the lens stretching out (see Figure 9-9).

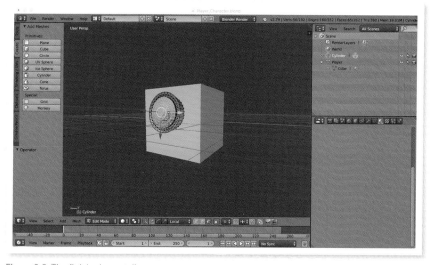

Figure 9-9: The finished eyestalk.

In Chapter 5, you made placeholder obstacles that the player had to avoid. The player knew these obstacles were bad because the coloring was red, which made the obstacle seem angry. In this case, you'll also use the color red. Select the cube and change the material's diffuse color to red.

Machines are also reflective because they have metal surfaces. Luckily, Blender makes it easy to add this reflectivity to our materials. In the Material tab, go down to where you see Mirror. Click the box next to Mirror so that it's selected. The Mirror drop-down list has the following options:

- **Reflectivity:** How reflective the material is. The more reflective it is, the more like a mirror it is. An object that is 1.0 reflective will just reflect what's around it.

- **A color choice:** What color the reflection will be tinted to; white is no tint. This will just be a block of color in the drop-down. By clicking that block, you'll be able to adjust the color.

- **Fresnel:** Determines how reflective the object is to materials at an angle from the material.

- **Blend:** How much the reflection blends into the material.

- **Depth:** How many reflections within reflections are allowed. If your scene has multiple reflected materials, and if the depth isn't high enough, those reflections won't show up on this material.

- **Max Distance:** How far away another object can be to be clearly seen in the reflection. (If the max distance is 0, it has no max distance.) If an object is past the max distance, it will be faded and blurry and will get more so until it can no longer be recognized in the mirror.

For the reflectivity of the metal, I suggest 0.110 with a blend of 1.25. This will create a nice metallic-looking object that will still look shiny and robotic. See Figure 9-10 as an example.

For the eye lens, you should follow the same steps as you did with the eyes earlier. The difference is that while the metal part of the lens is going to have a similar reflectivity to the metal body, the lens itself is made from a more reflective kind of glass or plastic. After you create a material for the metal part of the lens, select the lens parts of the object and create a new material and change its color to black (see Figure 9-11). After you do so, make sure that you up the reflectivity so that there is a much higher reflection in the lens compared to the body.

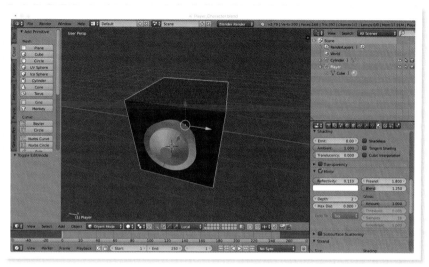

Figure 9-10: The enemy material.

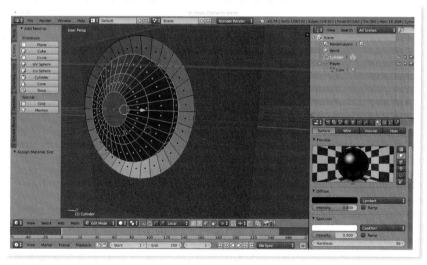

Figure 9-11: The lens.

After finishing the eye lens, rename the cube from player to enemy and parent the lens to that. Then save your project. You'll then have a completed grunt character for your videogame (like the one shown in Figure 9-12).

REMEMBER

Delete the light and camera in every new asset you create.

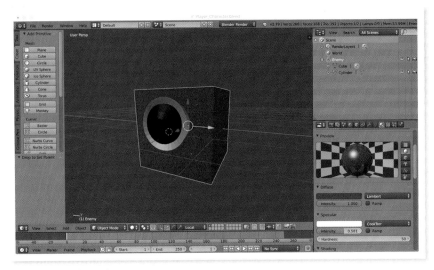

Figure 9-12: The finished grunt.

CREATING AN ENVIRONMENTAL HAZARD

You've created the characters in the game. Now it's time to design some scenery. You can use Blender to design all sorts of different environments and scenery, but here you'll design environmental hazards that the player has to avoid. The biggest difference between an environmental trap and an enemy is the size of the trap. The enemy character's size is similar to the characters' size and can be adjusted as needed, but in order for the environmental trap to work properly, it has to have specific measurements so that your characters can get through it.

In a 3D platformer, traps need to account for all three directions when you design them. If the trap needs to be avoided from the side, you need to think about how much distance it does cover and how to prevent players from jumping over it. If it's supposed to be jumped over, you need to design it with that in mind. It has to cover the entire section that the player needs to pass but leave enough room for the player to jump over.

Environmental hazards, similar to falls, act as non-enemy ways to kill the character and can help build the game to be more than just avoiding the enemies. The environmental trap for your game is one of my personal favorites in videogames, the crusher.

The crusher is a platform that the player needs to get past before the top of the platform comes smashing down and crushes the character. This obstacle requires two parts for it to work right: a bottom half for the player to climb on, and a top half that falls down on the player if they don't time it properly.

Follow these steps:

1. **Create a new file in Blender and save the file as crusher.blend.**

2. **Select the cube in the middle.**

3. **On the right side of the 3D viewer, click the small plus sign (+) in the dark box.**

4. **In the menu that appears, you see position, scale, and rotation sections each with the three different axis and numbers next to them. Change the X scale to 30, the Y scale to 3, and the Z scale to 0.5.**

   The size of the map on the *x*-axis is 30; this will prevent players from being able to go around it. The Z being equal to 0.5 will ensure that players will have to jump to just get on top of the platform — not much but a little bit. The Y being equal to 3 will force the player to land on the platform and, thus, in harm's way for a split second. This will force the player to time her movements even more carefully.

This will create a nice base (see Figure 9-13) to start from for the rest of the model. Part of the fun of this platform is creating something that forces the player to put himself in harm's way for a split second. It helps players learn the key to timing their actions. To make this even more difficult for the player, put the platform at a slightly higher height. This will really force the player to jump up to get past it, so it'll take slightly longer.

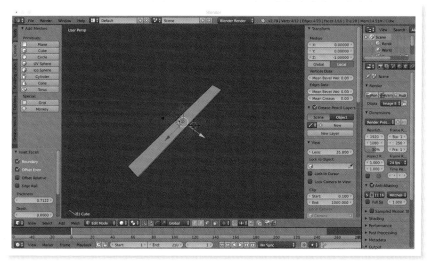

Figure 9-13: The base part of the platform.

The way to do that, while still keeping to the whole robot dystopian theme, is to make it even more obviously a platform. On the bottom of the platform that you created, inset a face and size it so that it's smaller than the platform's bottom and just big enough to look like a column of some sort for the platform (see Figure 9-14).

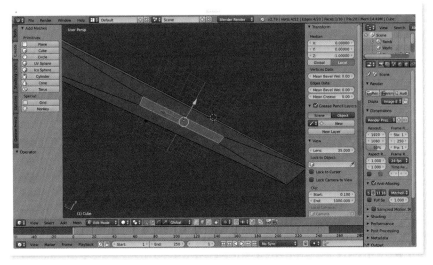

Figure 9-14: The bottom inset.

After you make the bottom inset, extrude out the inset face. The extrusion shouldn't be too great; otherwise, the character will be able to just go underneath the obstacle or it won't be able to jump over it. In this case, you should make the total height of the obstacle itself be equal to that of the character's height. From what we know, the character can jump higher than his own height. Because of this, the character will be able to make it over something that is the same height.

The obstacle's height thus far is 0.5. Because the character's height is 1, you know that the platform right now is half the character's height. So just extrude out until the bottom part of the platform is the same size as the top half of the platform (see Figure 9-15).

After you finish the bottom platform, it's time to work on the crusher part of this object. This will be the part of the platform that, when you animate it in Chapter 10, will come crashing down and kill the character if the character is on it. Luckily, you don't need to design this part from scratch. Because the platform and the crusher have to be the same size on the x-axis, at the very least you can just duplicate the bottom platform and rotate it 180 degrees on the y-axis so that it's facing downward. You also want to make sure that it's far enough away from the bottom platform so that the player character can actually jump and make it through the crusher without accidentally hitting the top. Drag the crusher part of the platform up high so that it's far enough away from the platform but still isn't too far away so that when it drops it isn't taking too long to get to a distance that would kill a player. If it's too close or too far, the game's difficulty can change dramatically. The crusher should look like Figure 9-16.

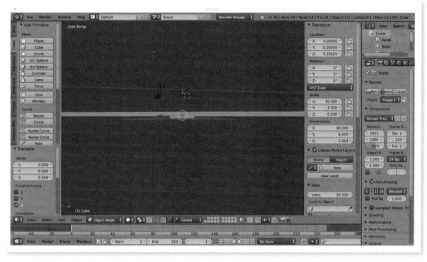

Figure 9-15: The finished bottom platform.

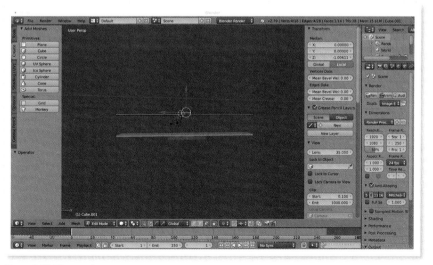

Figure 9-16: The crusher.

Although this would be enough to make the crusher, from a mechanical standpoint you want to actually create something that fits with the theme that you've set in the game. In this case, the theme is a robot dystopia, so on the top of the crusher you're going to add a little police light.

Using the Inset Face, Extrude, and Loop-Cut tools start building up a police light to put at the top of the crusher:

1. **Inset a face on the small area on the top of the crusher that used to be the platform bottom for the bottom half.**

2. **Scale that inset so that it looks closer to a square shape.**

3. **Move that inset line up along the z-axis so that there is a progressive climb to the next height.**

4. **Extrude and bring the extrusion up, giving some space in between to be the light itself.**

5. **Extrude again but go only a small distance up.**

6. **Extrude again, bringing it up slightly more and sizing it down a bit at the top so it gets smaller the farther up it goes.**

7. **Extrude again at the top to give it a nice flat top.**

8. **Using Alt-select, select the small extrusion from Step 5 and select all around it.**

9. **Extrude and use the x-axis and y-axis to expand the extrusion out so that it looks like a roof to the light (see Figure 9-17 for an example).**

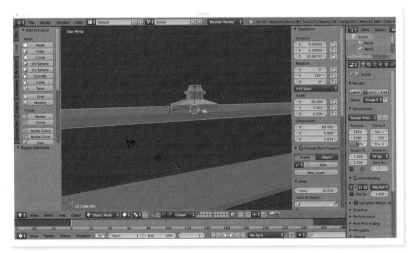

Figure 9-17: The light.

After you finish the top light, it's time to actually make the bottom part of the crusher to make it more intimidating. One of the most common ways to make the crusher look intimidating is by adding spikes to it, but this is a robot dystopia where most of the characters are cubes so spikes don't feel right in the environment. For this environment, a flat bottom crusher with some indents feels more appropriate, so that's what you're going to make.

REMEMBER
Save your project.

In order to create the necessary indents, you'll need to be able to extrude out on the bottom of the crusher only certain parts of the mesh as opposed to the whole bottom face. In order to do this, you need to create more faces. The best tool to do that with while still keeping quads is the Loop-Cut Slide tool.

You can just use the tool multiple times to create the indents needed, but there is actually a way to make multiple cuts at once with the Loop-Cut Slide tool. While the tool is still pink, you can roll the middle mouse button forward and back to create multiple lines that will all cut at once. Do this so that you cut six lines vertically across the bottom and horizontally across the bottom (see Figure 9-18).

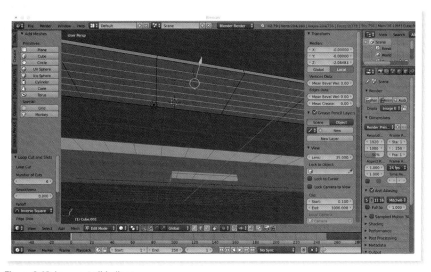

Figure 9-18: Loop-cut slide lines.

After you create the necessary lines, begin selecting every other face on the bottom of the mesh. That way, the bottom of the mesh will look like a checkerboard kind of pattern (see Figure 9-19). This will give you the ability to extrude only the faces you want to extrude. For this project, you only want to extrude these faces to give the crusher some sense of style and pattern.

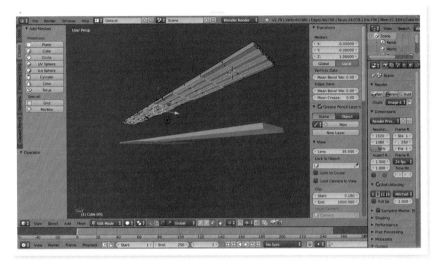

Figure 9-19: The checkerboard pattern at the bottom of the crusher.

After you have all the faces selected, you should extrude them out. As before, you don't want to extrude them out too much because you want to leave room for your player to get underneath, but you also want the size of the crusher to be notable in the game. Extrude the crusher sections out a little more than what you extruded the original platform out the first time. You'll notice now that all the extrusions will look like a bunch of rectangles. That's because you only pulled out the selected faces. The faces are still connected because of the shared vertices, but they'll look like they're slightly separated, which is mechanically not any different but helps build out the game's style.

After you finish the model for the crusher (see Figure 9-20), you have to also give it a material, similar to the enemy and player characters before. Red could still work for the crusher's color, but the model itself already looks intimidating without that much color. So, instead, I suggest choosing a much softer color and making only the police light red so that it stands out on the crusher.

Create a new material for the crusher and make it a kind of greenish gray to represent the mechanical nature of the crusher. Assign it to both the top and bottom of the crusher. Then, following the same steps as you did with the eyes, change the light at the top of the crusher to red to represent the light.

When you finish the crusher, like the one shown in Figure 9-21, save the project and create a new file for the next asset.

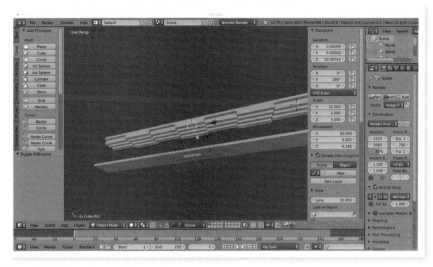

Figure 9-20: The crusher model complete.

You can also make objects transparent in Blender by going down to the Transparent section and selecting it so it's on. Then you just need to adjust the alpha. The lower the alpha, the less visible the player is.

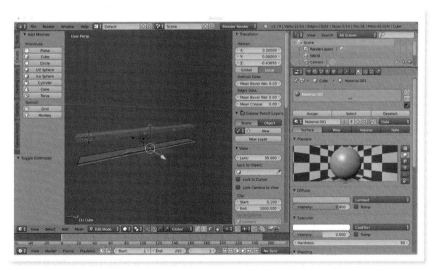

Figure 9-21: The crusher model complete.

CREATING THE MOVING PLATFORM

Platforms are a key part of platformers, for obvious reasons. One of the most common platforms in any platformer is the moving platform. Moving platforms are like regular platforms, but instead they move around. In the game that you created, you may remember that you never created a spot for a moving platform. This isn't entirely true. In the level, you created several planks that are across large gaps in the level. These spots were planned to be the locations for the moving platforms as opposed to the bridges that you were using earlier.

Moving platforms are discussed in more detail in the animation chapter where you're actually in charge of making the platforms move in your game. But right now, your goal is to create the base of the platform that you can animate later. Luckily, moving platforms are really simple to make.

Start by opening a new file in Blender and saving it as moving platform. blend. Select the cube in the middle of the grid and open the side window on the 3D view. Change the size of the moving platform to X=5, Y=5, and Z=0.5. This will create a platform large enough that your character can jump on and thin enough to look good as a platform. This would work as a platform but once again you want to be able to stylize this for your game.

Follow these steps:

1. **Go to Edit Mode.**

2. **Select the top and bottom faces.**

3. **Inset both faces to make a square in the middle.**

4. **Extrude the insets.**

5. **Using the Scale tool, move the insets closer together in the mesh.**

After you build the base for the model, change the material of it so it looks mechanical. You can even make the center part of the mesh look like glass. Simply go into Edit Mode, select the top and bottom insets, and change the color to blue and the transparency to 0.3 to 0.5, whichever you prefer. Also, put the reflections on for all the materials for the moving platform. This will create a nice moving platform for you to animate later, like the one shown in Figure 9-22.

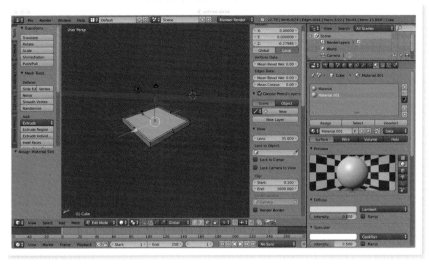

Figure 9-22: The moving platform.

CREATING THE COIN PICKUPS

The last thing you should create in this chapter are coins to take the place of the pickup items. When they're completed, the coins will rotate slowly and bounce up and down, but for now they'll just stay still. To start off, create a new file and name it Coins.blend. Delete the cube in the center, as well as the lights and camera. Coins are a good objective to pick up. We already associate coins with wealth and something to be desired (symbolically) so a coin, shown in Figure 9-23, is a great pickup item.

Follow these steps:

1. **Create a cylinder.**

2. **Rotate that cylinder 90 degrees on the *y*-axis.**

3. **Reshape the coin so it's thin and small.**

4. **Select the front and back faces.**

5. **Inset those faces.**

6. **Extrude and size the faces in.**

Figure 9-23: The coin's base.

Now, to give the coin some more personality, you want to add a hole in the middle of the coin that indicates its value. In this case, just the number one will do. This will require the use of a Boolean modifier. Booleans are ways to combine two different objects together, by unifying them, taking the parts where they intersect, or subtracting one from the other.

Follow these steps:

1. **Create a new cube.**

2. **Size the cube so it's tall and thin and looks like the number one.**

3. **Expand its size so that it will go through the coin (see Figure 9-24).**

4. **Select the coin.**

5. **Go to the Modifier tab in the Properties window.**

6. **From the Add Modifier drop-down, select Boolean.**

There a three different operations for Boolean to choose from:

- **Intersect:** Only keeps the parts of the meshes that touch each other.

- **Union:** Combines the two objects.

- **Difference:** Subtracts one object from the other.

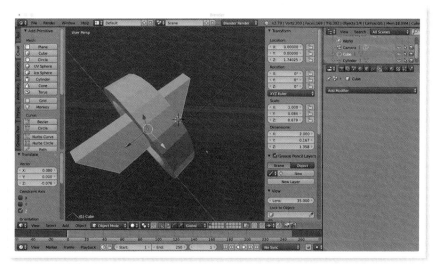

Figure 9-24: The number one intersecting.

7. Change the operation to Difference, as shown in Figure 9-25.

8. Change the Solve to Carve.

9. Underneath Object, click the empty slot and select Cube.

10. Press Apply and then delete the cube.

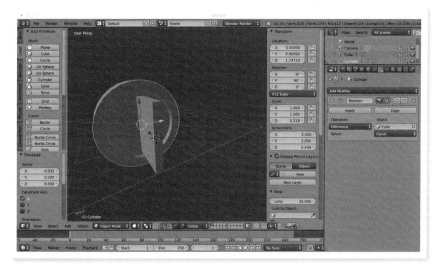

Figure 9-25: The Boolean modifier.

Now the coin will have a hole in it, giving it another reason to stand out in the level. After you finish building the coin, it's time to change the coin's color. As before, create a new material for the object and change it so it's both reflective and colorful (see Figure 9-26).

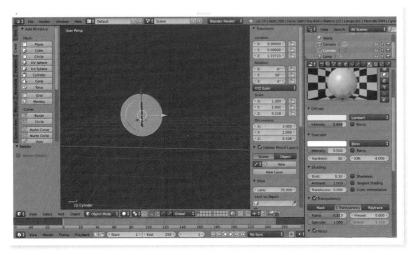

Figure 9-26: The hole cut out.

After you finish with the base model and color of the coin (like the one in Figure 9-27), see what changes you can make to the coin or any of the other objects created so that you can call it your own. In the case of the coin, I rounded out the edges and made it slightly transparent to help with the whole robot theme by making it seem more like a hologram that the character picks up.

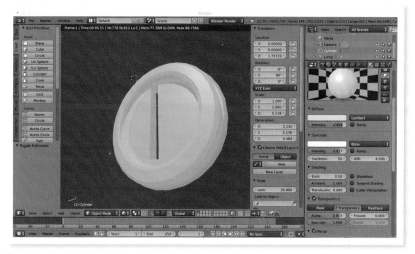

Figure 9-27: The finished coin.

CUSTOMIZING ON YOUR OWN

After you finish making and customizing some of the objects discussed in this chapter, try to make some more customizations to your level by adding signs or different characters or buildings. Asset creation is about creating any asset that you may need. This book only goes into the basic assets that make up your game, including the main character and a few of the enemies and environment hazards. Other ideas for objects you can model are mailboxes, trashcans, trees, signposts, and light posts.

The asset creation is where you can really make your game your own! So, think about what you can add to bring more life to your game. When you design your own game, come up with a list of assets before you begin. That way, when the time comes to build your own assets, you'll have a good idea of what to make and do.

Animating Your Characters

In this chapter, you'll learn the fundamentals of what goes into animation. In Chapter 9, you created models of characters and objects that are within your scene. Now it's time to breathe life into the game. You'll learn how to examine movement in life and how to translate that movement into your characters and game. You'll learn some animation terms such as *squash* and *stretch* and *anticipation*.

In Blender, you'll learn how to create and use keyframes, how to set up shape keys, and how to best animate within Blender. You'll also learn how to create animation loops that the game can refer to when the game is played. You'll have to create an animation loop for the non-playable characters and environment, but for your player character, you'll have to animate an idle pose, a walking motion, and a jump.

DEFINING ANIMATION

Animation is the illusion of life. It tricks the audience or player into believing that something is alive when it's just a series of rapidly moving pictures called *frames.* The goal of any animator is to make the viewer believe that the character or object is real, alive, breathing.

Animation has been around for more than a century. Over time, it has only become more elaborate and beautiful. Highly successful films and TV shows have been made using animation. Some live-action modern blockbusters use animation as a way to enhance their ability to tell their story. Most important, the videogame industry has thrived thanks to the advancements in animation. Without animation, videogames as we know them today would not be possible. Characters such as Mario and Sonic would never have come into being if animation weren't a key part of the videogame industry.

Today, with the use of 3D animation software, games can create vast and wonderful stories and capture the imaginations of millions of people. Animation has done a lot to help push the field of game development forward. Now one of the best fields for an animator to be a part of is game design. The two media — games and animation — are linked together and help push one another in new and exciting directions.

LEARNING ANIMATION

The most important thing you can do in animation is to *study everything.* Even if you're just creating the animations for a game, there is so much to learn and understand about the world around you before you can animate it.

How can you replicate life if you don't understand how life works? How can you bring a game world to life if you're unwilling to examine what life looks like in the real world?

With the limited processing power back in the arcade game days, each sprite had sprites to work with, so the animators had to find workarounds. Even today, some of the techniques they used, such as motion blur, are used in modern games to help give the punches and kicks more power despite not changing how fast the actual character is moving.

So, how do you examine motion and translate that motion into the game? Is it as simple as watching a person walking frame by frame and drawing each frame? The truth is that an accurate depiction of motion can only get you so far in animation. Animation isn't about re-creating motion exactly. It's about capturing the feeling of the motion.

Understanding the mechanical motion of a person walking is important in animation, but the most important thing for any animator to understand, in any medium, is that the feeling behind the motion is actually far more important to animating than the motion itself. There have been many motion-capture games and films over the years, some of them far better than others. But the problem that many motion-capture studios face is that the animation recorded with the motion capture often feels stiff and unnatural, despite being literally recorded from life. This is due to a concept called the uncanny valley.

The *uncanny valley* is the feeling you get when you watch or see something that is

REMEMBER

The goal of your game is to immerse the player. Some of the best games you've played do this without your even realizing it. Mario's world feels alive because no decision was made lightly — from how the Goombas move to how Mario jumps, everything in that game's animation was done by bringing a living place to the player. Sonic's running animation with the feet disappearing to only show what looks like a blur of motion attached to the bottom of the body was an animation choice — his whole gimmick was speed, so the animators made his running sprite look like it was moving at super-fast speeds to sell the player on that feeling. Fighting games especially use animation to their advantage by taking into account how we perceive punches and kicks in real life, especially when watching expert fighters like those depicted in the games. In the original Street Fighter, punches could take as little as five frames to complete. That's less than a second per punch, but the animation feels smooth and right because the developers knew how to make the punch feel right.

very close to being lifelike or human, but something feels just a slight bit off. I liken it to coming home to your house and finding that something — you're not sure what is — is just a slight bit too far to the left of where it was earlier. It fills you with a sense of unease. In animation, it makes you see the animation as stiff or robotic. The motion just feels wrong.

Humans have a very keen ability to recognize other humans. We understand universal body language because we can see the small details in a person's movement. We can always tell when something is human and when something isn't, and that's why extremely realistic characters don't hit the same level of attachment as some of the more stylized characters do. The uncanny valley occurs only when something looks close to human but isn't perfect. The less human something looks, the more at ease we are with them, but when something passes through the uncanny valley, we're able to relieve that uneasiness.

REMEMBER

The most important thing for you to animate right is the *feelings* behind the character's motion, not just the character's motion itself.

One of the best examples of this is the character Wall-E from the movie by the same name. Despite Wall-E and Eve clearly being machines with limited expressions, the audience was able to relate to the character because, instead of animating the characters to be as human as possible, the directors animated what the character was *feeling* not what the character was doing.

ANIMATING A FEELING

As a human, you know when something feels off. The best way to counteract this feeling is by animating the character so that the character looks how it feels. All the emotions should feel very different even though multiple emotions can be expressed in similar ways. Anger and sadness may look similar in real life, but if you don't push the character's expressiveness, these characters will never capture the minds of the players.

Here's a summary of some common feelings you may want to animate:

- **Happiness:** Happiness is a very light emotion. You feel like you weigh nothing. You may even have a skip to your step. Characters who are happy often stand up tall and move at a much brisker pace. Think of happiness like a freshly blown-up balloon. It's larger than life, and yet still feels very light.

- **Sadness:** Sadness is the exact opposite of happiness. When you're sad, you feel like the weight of the world is pulling you down. Each step or movement is strained and heavy. Sadness is a heavy and slow emotion. Characters who are sad might move more slowly and have their heads down.

- **Anger:** Anger is a large emotion, too. Everything feels tighter when you're angry. It feels as if the world is crashing down and you're just pushing back. Anger is a very large but precise emotion. It's driven.

- **Fear:** Fear is possibly the oddest of the emotions. When you're afraid, everything just feels bigger than you are. You feel small. You may move slowly in one moment, but run away in another. Fear is a frantic emotion, with very quick changes.

When you animate your characters, you have to consider not just what the character is doing but what the character feels like he's doing. The human eye has been trained to recognize natural movement. No matter how hard you try, you'll never be able to animate something that looks 100 percent like a human. This is why it's important to focus on how motion *feels.*

USING THE SQUASH-AND-STRETCH TECHNIQUE

Imagine slapping your hand against a hard surface. It feels like your hand is expanding out and snapping back into shape all at once when it makes contact. In reality, the skin on the hand may expand out a little and snap back into place, but it's barely visible — not nearly to the extent that it feels like when it happens. When you animate a scene, you want that feeling to come across more, so you exaggerate the motions to match the feeling rather than the actual motion. In animation terms, this technique is called *squash and stretch.*

A technique pioneered by Ub Iwerks and Walt Disney, squash and stretch gives weight and feeling to the characters. Before squash and stretch, animators never really paid attention to consistency. Characters would stretch their limbs out as needed, because they could, but this gave the impression that the shape and volume of the characters weren't consistent. It never gave the right feeling of a character actually existing in a real environment. Squash and stretch aims to keep the volume and shape of the object consistent even when the object expands or distorts it in extreme ways.

Squash is when a character slams against something. The body becomes wider and shorter to emphasize the impact. Think of a ball hitting the ground or your hand slapping a hard surface. To help reinforce the impact, the animator squishes the character down as if it were a balloon and something is pushing down on it. Because the character is expanding out, you also have to make the character shorter to keep the volume of the character consistent.

Stretch is the opposite of squash. Think about a ball or car moving really fast or someone swinging a baseball bat. Stretch elongates the object, making it thinner and giving the object the feeling of movement. Think of stretch as a kind of lag. One part of the object is moving, but part of it is still trying to catch up, so stretching occurs. In real life, objects are solid, so they don't distort — but it feels like they *should* be distorting. When something moves fast, it feels like it *should* be stretching,

One of the best ways to practice squash and stretch is to do a bouncing-ball animation. Rubber balls already distort slightly when they hit the ground, but in animation you need to exaggerate that motion. Follow these steps:

1. **On a pad of sticky notes, draw a circle at the top of the last note in the pad.**

2. **Note by note, draw the ball slowly going down toward the ground.**

3. **Stretch out the ball in the middle so that it looks more like an oval going toward the ground.**

4. **When the ball touches the ground, keep the bottom of the ball touching the bottom of the sticky note.**

5. **Slowly expand the ball out into a horizontal oval shape.**

6. **When the ball is a horizontal oval, begin snapping it back to a circle, and then just before it's a circle begin to bring the ball up again.**

7. **Stretch out the ball as it goes up.**

8. **Slowly have the ball snap back into a circle and then stop.**

The total animation should only be about ten frames, but the result will be a simple animation of a ball hitting the ground and bouncing back up, giving you a perfect example of squash and stretch in motion.

BUILDING ANTICIPATION

In animation, every motion needs to be exaggerated. That goes for the lead-up into a motion as well. *Anticipation* is the pre-action to a motion. When you jump, you first have to bend down. When you punch someone, you pull your fist back slightly. In animation, these anticipation moments help give the character a sense of realism.

No one just does an action — there is always a half-second delay. When you animate these moments, the character's anticipation is also exaggerated. Think of fighting games. When a character throws a punch, there is a slight pause before the punch is thrown. This pause is even more exaggerated when it's supposed to be more powerful. When you animate your characters, you should keep this anticipation in mind. Characters don't just jump up or attack. There has to be a moment of anticipation to really sell the idea that these characters exist.

That said, you don't want the delay to be too long. Otherwise, these motions will kill the flow of gameplay. So, when you're animating your characters, you have to keep in mind both the gameplay and the animation.

ANIMATING YOUR PLAYER CHARACTER

The first thing you should animate for your game is your player character because it requires the most animations. Unlike the other objects or characters, the player character's movements directly relate to what the player is doing at any given time. The enemy characters or hazards have specific animation loops that never change — they just repeat continuously.

The player character needs to do different things depending on what the player needs:

- **An idle animation:** Most games these days don't have the characters just stand still on the screen when the player isn't moving. You're creating living characters for the players to control. If the character stands still, this can break that immersion.

  In the original Sonic the Hedgehog game, SEGA used the idle animation to reinforce the personality of the main character as a "too cool" speedster. If players don't move Sonic, he'll begin to tap his foot impatiently, waiting for the player to make a movement. And if players wait long enough, Sonic will even jump off the edge of the level out of impatience and leave!

- **A walking animation:** The most standard animation in the game, movement animations have existed since the days of Pac-Man. If a character is just floating around the screen, it breaks player immersion. Adding a walk cycle for whenever the character moves helps give life to your character.

- **A jump animation:** This animation adds more to how the character moves around and helps reinforce the idea of the character as being alive. When you jump, you don't just move vertically. Jump motions add animation to a jump, to help sell the illusion of playing as a real character.

The main character of the game you're creating in this book is a box (see Figure 10-1), so the character's actual movement is limited — but it's still possible to give a box life and feeling. (Consider the Luxo Jr. lamp from Pixar as an example of how to get feeling from an inanimate object.) For your game, you'll focus on a way to get only the basic movement of the character, keeping in mind that the techniques and tools that you'll be using can also be used to create far more extensive ranges of motion.

Figure 10-1: Boxo!

To create *biped characters* (characters that stand on two limbs) or simply characters with limbs, think about how to rig your character, creating bones/ armatures that will give you the ability to move your character's limbs. Rigging isn't complicated, but it can be confusing for first-time users so look through Blender's website for a comprehensive introduction to rigging.

USING SHAPE KEYS

Blender separates editing from object manipulation through the two different modes. The problem is that you aren't able to animate changing the character's shape with the vertices, edges, or faces within Blender. Blender's animation tools are limited to Object Mode (and Pose Mode through rigging). Although you can animate many parts of the object (including the textures and modifiers, as you'll learn later in this chapter), you can't animate changes made within Edit Mode without an particular Blender extension. And even then, the animation is limited and finicky at best.

So, with a character as simple as a box, how are you supposed to animate the character so that it feels alive and moving? Luckily, Blender has an answer for this in the form of shape keys.

Shape keys are different variations on the shape of the same object. They allow you to mark changes in your edit and adjust the influence of those changes on a scale from 0 influence to 1 influence. You can have multiple shape keys on the same object, but when both shape keys are being used at the same time, the object distorts to the midpoint of the two different shape keys. Shape keys are useful tools for creating things like facial animations because you can use multiple shape keys to affect different parts of the face, such as the eyes and the mouth. You can also combine shape keys to create more complex emotions.

For the player character, you'll be using shape keys to help bring to life their movement within the scene. Because the character designs are so simplistic in nature, the way the character moves and expresses has been reduced. But you can still rely on the cartoony nature of the style to help bring the character to life.

First, you need to create a shape key:

1. **Select the object that you want.**

2. **Go to the Object Data tab in the Properties section of the window.**

3. **Scroll down to Shape Keys.**

4. **On the right side, click the plus sign (+) button twice.**

    This creates a base shape key that all the other shape keys will use as a reference. Clicking it a second time will also create your first shape key (see Figure 10-2).

5. **Select Key 1 and switch to Edit Mode.**

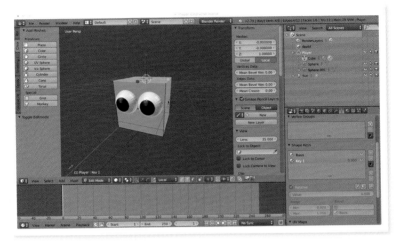

Figure 10-2: Creating shape keys.

Now whatever changes you make in Edit Mode will automatically be recorded into Key 1. All the changes you make will also have no effect on the base key or any other shape key made after this.

Start off by adjusting one of the faces and switching back to Object Mode. When you do, you'll notice that the change resets itself. This is because the shape keys are only active when you want them to be active. By adjusting the value to the right of the key from 0 to 1, you can determine how much the shape changes to match the shape key. At a value of 1, the shape changes to match the shape key entirely.

Now switch back to Edit Mode and adjust the shape so that the cube looks like it's squatting down (see Figure 10-3).

Figure 10-3: The first shape key.

Note how the eyes aren't moving to match the shape key. This is because the eyes are a separate object from the body and are not affected by changes done within editing. The eyes are attached to the total body, not the mesh, so changes to the mesh will have no effect on the eyes. But don't worry — you'll be editing and animating the eyes soon.

After you finish the first shape key (see Figure 10-4), double-click that shape key and rename it Walk. This shape key will serve as the primary animation for your walk cycle. After renaming the shape key, reset the influence to 0 and create two more shape keys by clicking the plus sign (+) button. Rename these two shape keys Right Turn and Left Turn, and select either one.

1. **Enter Edit Mode.**

2. **Select the top face.**

3. **Use the rotate tool to rotate that face slightly to the side indicated by the name.**

4. **Return to Object Mode and repeat this process for the other side.**

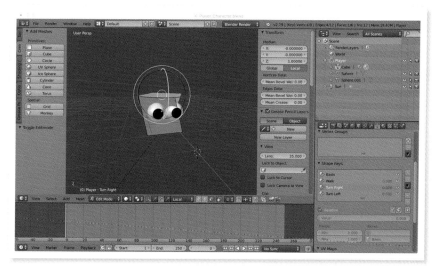

Figure 10-4: The first shape key.

BREAKING DOWN YOUR PLAYER CHARACTER'S ANIMATION

In most animations, including the ones you'll be doing later in this chapter for the game, you do only one major animation, with each individual part of the animation flowing into the others naturally over time. This isn't the case for your player character, because you need multiple animations in one Timeline so that your game can refer to them in Chapter 12 when you import you characters.

CREATING A KEYFRAME

Keyframes are the specific points in your animation that indicate movement. In old animations, they would be the major points in movement the character makes with the in-between frames being the frames that go from one keyframe to the next. In 3D animation, keyframes act much the same except that the computer automatically calculates the in-between frames.

There are three ways to create a keyframe in Blender:

- At the bottom of the Timeline there is a red button. This is for automatic key framing. When you move along the Timeline and then adjust the character when autokeying is on, it will automatically record the movement. It will also record any other changes within the Scene window, but it's limited to only changes made within the scene, and not outside of the scene, so shapeless and material changes are not recorded by autokeying.

- The Animation tab to the left of the screen has an Insert and Delete Keyframe button. When you want to insert a keyframe, you click Insert Keyframe, and a menu pops up indicating all the different types of keyframes you can add, from the transform tools to the modifiers.

- The final way to insert a keyframe is to hover over what you want the keyframe to affect and pressing the I button on the keyboard. This creates a keyframe that affects the selected aspect of the object and can give you the control of inserting the keyframe via the animation menu while still giving the convenience of the autokeying. This can also affect modifiers and materials as well.

REMEMBER

The Delete Keyframe button is a great way to delete keyframes that you placed by accident. The other way is to use something called a dope sheet (see Chapter 12), or to right-click the part of the animation affected by the keyframe (highlighted yellow) and click Delete Keyframe.

BEGINNING YOUR ANIMATION

Now that you've set up the shape keys and understand how key framing works, it's time to start animating your character. Because this is your player character, you should figure out how much time each pose or motion will have for the animation.

For the idle animation, you want about 3 to 5 seconds; for the walk cycle, only about 2 to 3 seconds; and the jump animation should be only 1 to 2 seconds. If you use the max time for all the animations, the total frame count should be around 300 frames. Be sure to give some time in between each animation to prevent bleed over from one animation to another.

REMEMBER

The character is actually facing toward the right of the screen right now, so to make sure the character is facing forward, change the Z rotation to –90. Follow these steps:

Let's start with the idle animation. In this animation, the actual motion the character will make will start when the player is idle for 3 seconds. After 3 seconds, the character will look around to the left and right side and then wait for another 3 seconds before doing so again. Three seconds in an animation that is 30 frames per second means that the animation will begin at frame 90.

1. **At frame 0, insert keyframes for all the transform tools, as well as for all the shape keys.**

   When you do this they should all highlight yellow (see Figure 10-5).

2. **Go to frame 90 and insert frames the same way.**

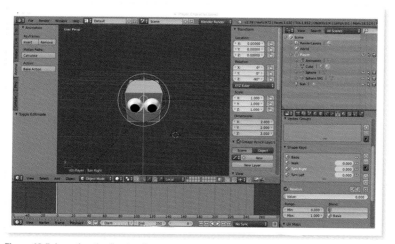

Figure 10-5: Inserting the first keyframe.

3. **Skipping 20 frames, change either the right or left turns to 1.**

4. **Insert keyframes.**

5. **Move two frames forward.**

6. **Insert keyframes.**

7. **At frame 120, change the shape keys to 0.**

8. **Insert keyframes.**

9. **Repeat steps 2 through 6.**

10. **At frame 150, change all the shape keys back to 0.**

11. **Insert keyframes.**

Save!

ANIMATING THE CHARACTER'S EYES

You don't want your character's eyes to fall out of its head (see Figure 10-6) in your game. Because of this, your player character's eyes also have to move an animate to match the body animation. The problem is that animating the eyes individually (see Figure 10-7) can be tedious. Plus, it may not guarantee that the eyes will rotate the right way.

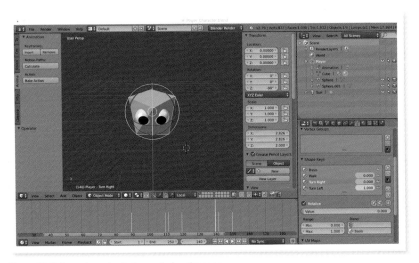

Figure 10-6: Your character before rotating the eyes.

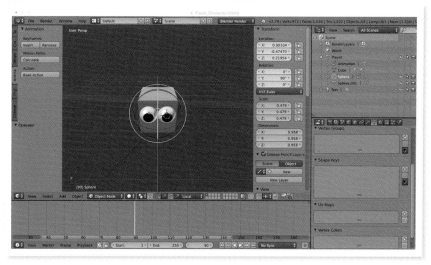

Figure 10-7: A first attempt at rotating the eyes.

The best way to fix this problem is to add a way to control both eyes at once while still matching the rotation of the cube's shape. Adding an empty (as in Figure 10-8) that you can parent the eyes to will guarantee that the eyes will move at the same rotation, and you can even make it so the rotation of the empty matches the rotation of the body.

1. **Create a new empty.**

2. **Rename the empty "eye control."**

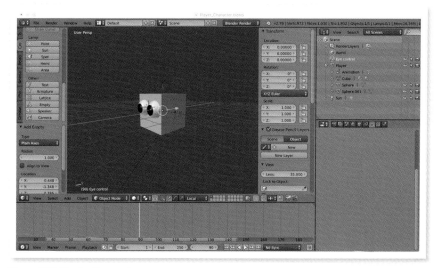

Figure 10-8: Placing the empty.

3. **Change the position of the empty to (0,0,0).**

   Because the cube is the same cube from opening up Blender, the origin point is currently located at (0,0,0). By moving the empty there, the eyes will be controlled and rotate along the same rotation that the cube is distorting.

4. **Parent the eye control to the cube.**

5. **Parent the eyes to the empty.**

This will make it so that the eyes will rotate together along the same axis that the box is distorting and turning on. Now it's time to animate the eyes, but a new problem arises: When the character turns, the faces on the top actually get smaller when they turn so the eyes will be popping out. You can fix this by adjusting the rotation and position of the eyes so that they get slightly closer as the character turns (see Figure 10-9). Just be sure to match the eye turning and adjustment with the keyframes of Boxo turning.

Figure 10-9: Boxo turning with adjusted eyes.

So you don't have to match the XYZ every time, go to the spots where the eyes are in their starting positions and put those keyframes in first while the eyes are still there. Then do the eyes in their new positions when they turn.

WORKING ON THE WALK CYCLE

The next movement on the list is the walk cycle. Although this may be more difficult to animate for bipeds or quadrupeds, because the player character is just a single box the walk cycle is actually much simpler to animate than the idle animation.

To start off, you'll want to make sure that your character is in its starting pose before you begin. That way all the animations start out with the same base and don't rely on any other animations to come before or after, giving more power to the player to control the character without breaking the illusion.

Follow these steps:

1. **Skip ahead 20 or so frames to give each section of animation room in front and behind (see Figure 10-10).**

Figure 10-10: Setting up the next section for animation.

2. **Set the starting keyframe here.**

3. **Move ten frames.**

4. **Change the walk shape key to 1.**

5. **Set a keyframe.**

6. **Move ten frames.**

7. **Change the walk shape key to 0.**

8. **Set a keyframe.**

9. **Repeat steps 3 through 8 one more time.**

After you finish the walk cycle (like the one in Figure 10-11), it's time to adjust the eyes so that they don't remain still while the body moves. Like before, match the eyes to the motion of the body using the keyframes. This one should be easier because all it requires is to move the eyes up and down to match the changing of the mesh. This will give the illusion of the character moving up and down as they walk (like the one in Figure 10-12).

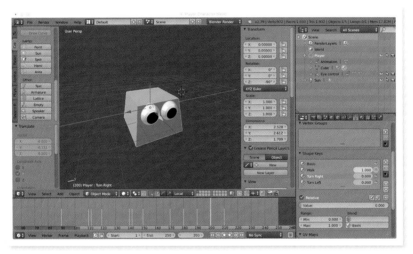

Figure 10-11: The finished walk.

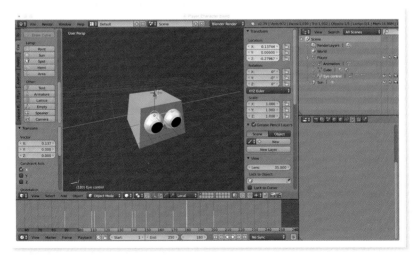

Figure 10-12: The finished walk with eyes.

Because you've already coded the character walking in the game and moving forward and backward, you don't have to animate that movement. The character will already move forward, left, right, and backward. If you were to animate that sort of movement in the game, the character could move in the wrong direction or extremely fast. Whenever you make a character whose movement you control, you should have the character remain still while still looking like it's moving.

If you find this difficult, try creating a large circle and placing it at the bottom of your character's feet. Think of this circle as a treadmill that your character can't get off. Parenting the character to the circle will allow you to move around the circle without causing any problems and give you a clear idea of the boundary when you animate.

JUMPING

Jumping is the final animation you'll need to do for this character, but it's also the hardest and probably the one that you'll have to adjust at later points to better fit the jumping in your game. When a character jumps, you have to show both the anticipation of the jump and the jump itself, all while not moving the character too much because of how the character interacts with the game. Animating the character to jump higher will cause the character in the game to jump even higher than what you want him to be able to jump. To fix this problem, you'll also have to make another new shape key (see Figure 10-13).

Up until this point, you've mainly been working with squash animation. Now it's time for you to work with stretch animation. To give the appearance of jumping fast, the character's body should elongate as if part of the body is being left behind. In practice, this should help sell the idea that the character is jumping high and fast because, as the shape key returns to normal, the box will be hitting its full height, making it seem like the box jumped up fast to reach its height. This gives the illusion of mass and life to the character and the world, further immersing the player in the world you've created.

REMEMBER

The mass of the object must remain consistent in order to succeed in giving the audience the feeling of weight. What is taken or given to height or weight must inversely be given back.

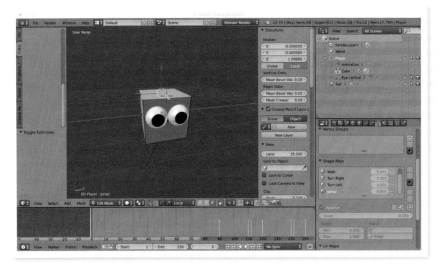

Figure 10-13: The jump shape key.

Follow these steps to make a jump animation for the character:

1. **Starting on frame 230, place your first keyframe down.**

2. **To not make the anticipation too long of a wait, make sure that the crouch down (using the walk shape key for the crouch) takes only about five frames to get to and only an extra two to hold.**

3. **On frame 240, switch out the squash from the walking shape key and instead use the jump shape key.**

4. **Have Boxo return to his normal shape on frame 245.**

The last thing you need to adjust is the eyes themselves. Up until this point, the eyes have just been moved or rotated around, but now it's time to apply the squash-and-stretch animation to the player character's eyes as well.

The eyes should stretch in a similar fashion to the box (see Figure 10-14). That way, people know that the body and eyes are intact. Using the eye control, change the shape and position of the eye to match the pose in the animation (see Figure 10-15).

When Boxo returns to its normal shape, the eyes should also return to their normal shape and size. Match the eyes to the keyframes and then save your finished character so that you can import them into Unity in Chapter 12.

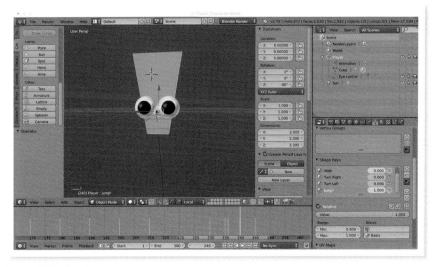

Figure 10-14: Boxo jumping.

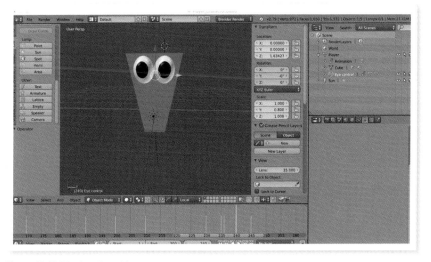

Figure 10-15: The jumping with eyes.

ANIMATING THE ENEMY GRUNT

These are the Goombas and the Koopa Troopas in your platformer. Arguably the second most important characters in the game, the enemy characters are just as important to think about when animating as the player characters are. In the case of this game, the enemies are all robots (like the one in Figure 10-16), so when you're thinking about their movements, you have to keep that in mind.

The player character is more organic in this game, so its movements are more fluid and rubbery to give that extra sense of life. Creating a distinction between the player and the enemies can go beyond just aesthetic differences in color or shape. You can even use the animation to help highlight the differences between the player and the enemy. The player character is fluid, so the enemy should be stiff; the player moves more sporadically, so the enemy should have a consistent movement; and so on.

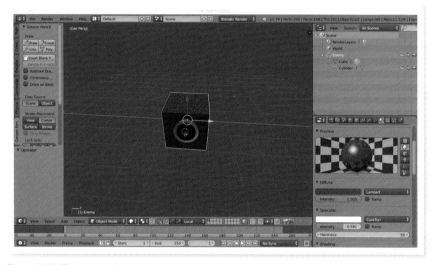

Figure 10-16: The enemy character.

You need the enemy character to walk back and forth across the stage in a circle. Where the enemy placeholder is currently located, you'll place the enemy character so that it can move back and forth in that spot. The goal of the enemy character is to present a challenge that the player must overcome or avoid. In 2D platformers, the character will move toward and away from the player in a pattern. Because there were only two directions that the player can move in, this posed a challenge that the players would have to solve. In a 3D platformer, the character moving only forward and backward doesn't pose as much of a threat to the player because the player could easily just move to the side and avoid the enemy. To present an adequate challenge to the player, you must use the animation of the enemy to block a path that the player must get by. In this case, the character will be moving along the x-axis.

You know that the total size of the platforms is 30. As you're placing the character at the center of the platform, that means from the center point of the animation, the character travels 15 units on either side of the center point, which is 0. That means the two X positions that the character will be traveling between are 15 and –15.

Follow these steps to create a moving enemy grunt:

1. **Set the X Location to –15.**

2. **At frame 0, set the keyframes of the location, rotation, and scale tools.**

   See Figure 10-17 for the starting position example.

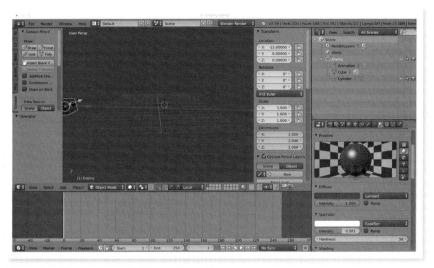

Figure 10-17: The enemy grunt in his starting position.

3. **Determine how fast you want the character to move across the stage.**

   For example, if you want your character to move across the stage in 3 seconds, that would be 90 frames. How fast the character is moving across the stage affects the difficulty because players will have to avoid hitting it.

4. **Go to the frame you determined in Step 3 and set the X position to 15.**

5. **Insert a keyframe.**

   Now instead of having the character just turn around and go the other way to create a loop, you're going to take advantage of the 3D environment by having the character move in a square rather than in a straight line.

6. **Go up by ten frames.**

7. **Change the rotation on the Z to 90 degrees.**

8. **Insert a keyframe for the rotation only.**

9. **Insert another keyframe five frames earlier for the position.**

    See Figure 10-18 as an example.

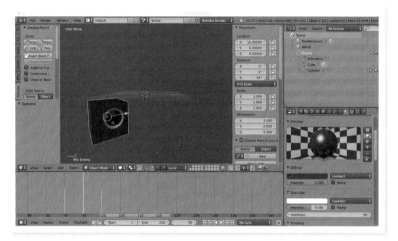

Figure 10-18: The grunt character rotating in position 2.

10. **Under the assumption that the frame in Step 4 was 90, go to frame 115. (Otherwise just add 25 to whatever frame you used in Step 4.)**

11. **Change the Y position to 5.**

    See Figure 10-19 as an example.

12. **Insert a keyframe.**

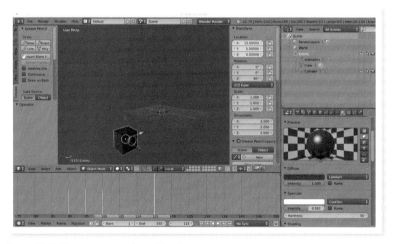

Figure 10-19: The enemy grunt in position 3.

The next steps repeat this same process by having the character turn around by 90 degrees in ten frames and move back to −15 in the same amount of frames you had the character move in the original movement (90 frames from before the turn in the example). When the character gets back to −15 frames on the X, have it rotate one more time and move to the Y position 0.

If you use the 90 frames as the time it takes for the character to cross the stage, then the total frames of this animation should be 240. This will create an enemy character that will be moving back and forth on the game platform that the player will have to avoid, like the one shown in Figure 10-20.

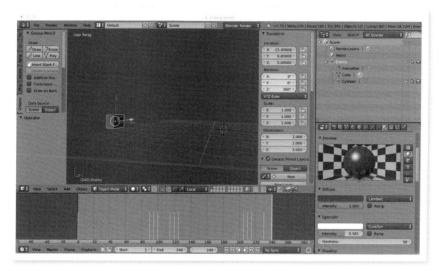

Figure 10-20: The final enemy grunt animation.

ANIMATING THE ENVIRONMENTAL HAZARD

The environmental hazard that you created was a crusher, like the one in Figure 10-21, which means you need to animate it falling down onto the platform after a certain amount of time, pause there for a moment, and then rise up again for the player to get through.

Part of the benefit of the crusher as a hazard that the player has to overcome is that the model already will expand the entirety of the width of the stage, so it forces players to go through it to get to the end. Unfortunately, that means that in order to give players a chance to get through the crusher, you have to provide players with enough time to jump through it. For this one, 3 seconds should be plenty of time for the player to make it through the crusher without being hit by it.

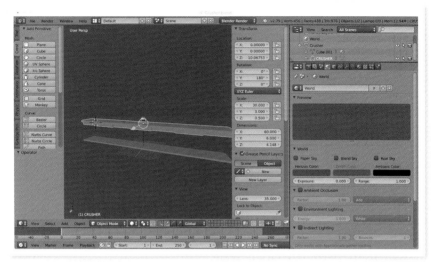

Figure 10-21: The crusher.

Follow these steps to create an obstacle that will provide a challenge for the player without being punishing:

1. **Set a keyframe at the beginning of the animation.**

2. **Go 90 frames and insert another keyframe (position).**

   The next thing you have to decide is how fast the crusher will fall before hitting the bottom and stopping. For this, ten frames should be more than enough for the falling animation.

3. **Go to frame 100 and adjust the Z position until the top of the crusher is touching the bottom of the crusher.**

4. **Insert a keyframe for the position at frame 100, and then add another keyframe at frame 120.**

   This will ensure that the crusher stays in its position for a short period of time and prevents the player from getting past it.

5. **Go to frame 140 and move the crusher back to its starting position on the *z*-axis.**

   To give the crusher more impact when it hits the bottom platform, try adding some squash and stretch or even have it bounce a little bit upon hitting the surface of the platform. By adding some squash and stretch, it will make the falling of the crusher seem even faster and the impact feel like it hits even harder. By adding a few frames after where the crusher bounces up and falls back down into place, you give the crusher more gravity. Even a brick bounces when it drops — it doesn't bounce *much,* and it'll even break, but there is a slight impact reverb, and animating that into your game will help sell the idea of weight.

6. **Check frames 90 and 100 to make sure that there are keys set for their scale.**

7. **Go to frame 95.**

8. **Change the Y scale to 2.7 and the Z scale to 0.8.**

9. **Insert a keyframe.**

10. **Go to frame 102 and make sure the scale is correct.**

    The X scale should be 30, the Y scale should be 3, and the Z scale should be 0.5.

11. **Insert a keyframe for the scale.**

12. **In frame 100, change the X scale to 30.68, the Y scale to 3.44, and the Z scale to 0.42.**

    This will create a squash-and-stretch effect that will give the falling of the crusher more impact when it hits. It doesn't change anything except the shape of the mesh, but that small change does a lot to give the impression of power.

    Next, you'll animate the impact reverb of the crusher.

13. **In frame 100, move the crusher down on the *z*-axis so that the bottom of the crusher is touching the platform.**

14. **Insert a keyframe for the position.**

15. **Go to frame 102 and move the crusher slightly up on the *z*-axis.**

16. **Insert a position keyframe.**

17. **Go to frame 104.**

18. **Move the position of the crusher down and scale it so that the Z scale is smaller and the X and Y scales are larger, but scale it less than what you did for frame 30 in Step 12.**

    This represents the object coming to rest. It's still hitting the platform hard and distorting a slight bit, but by distorting less this time, it gives the illusion that the mesh's landing is slowing down.

19. **Insert a keyframe.**

20. **Move to frame 105.**

21. **Move the crusher up a slight bit so that it's just off of the platform and change its scale back to normal (see Step 10).**

22. **Insert a keyframe.**

23. **Move to frame 106.**

24. **Move the crusher to the platform and insert a keyframe.**

When you're done, you'll have a finished crusher animation like the one in Figure 10-22.

Figure 10-22: The finished crusher animation.

ANIMATING A MOVING PLATFORM

The moving platform is probably the easiest thing to animate within Blender. Unlike the enemy character, which had rotation and moved in multiple directions, or the crusher, which had to have a delay in it, the moving platform just goes back and forth in one direction.

The moving platform is supposed to act as a sort of bridge for the character to use to jump across some chasms within the game. It should only move a limited distance, though, so players will still have to jump onto it and off of it to reach their goals, again presenting them with a challenge that they must overcome within the game.

Following the example given in Figure 10-23, you're going to animate the moving platform moving across the y-axis:

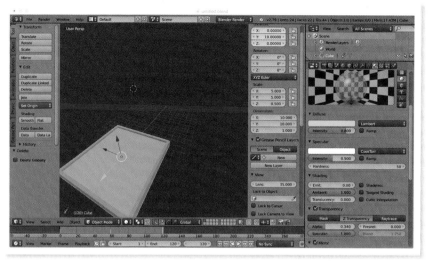

Figure 10-23: The moving platform.

1. **Go to Frame 0.**

2. **Set the Y position to 10.**

   The total range of movement for this platform is 20 units.

3. **Insert a keyframe.**

4. **Go to frame 120.**

5. **Insert a keyframe.**

6. **Go to frame 60.**

7. **Set the Y position to –10.**

8. **Insert a keyframe.**

9. **Change the end frame count to 120.**

   After you make the animation, you'll notice that the platform never stops moving. This could be a problem because you'll want to give players at least a moment or two when the platform stops to give the player time to jump on the platform. Five frames of waiting should be enough.

10. **Go to frame 5.**

11. **Change the Y position to 10.**

12. **Insert a keyframe.**

13. **Go to frame 65.**

14. **Change the Y position to –10.**

15. **Insert a keyframe.**

You won't need to add a pause after frame 120 because the animation will automatically loop to a pause as it is.

ANIMATING THE COINS

The last thing you need to animate for this game are the coins, shown in Figure 10-24, for the player to pick up. You're going to animate the coins to spin and bounce up and down slowly on the game level. This will give them a nice effect within the game and make them stick out for players.

You should animate objectives to move, even slightly, to help them stand out from the background. For objects that you want to be picked up, you should always give small indications to the players that these *can* be picked up. Giving the item a highlight when the player passes near it, making it a different color, or giving it a small in-place animation are all things that can help add to the idea that these items can be picked up. Because these are pickup items spread throughout the game, making them float slightly off the ground is a good way to make them stand out to the player while not making them threatening or getting them confused with the enemies.

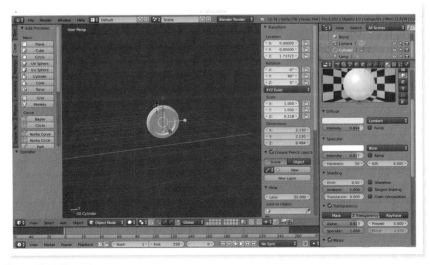

Figure 10-24: The coin.

First, let's animate the object spinning. The total animation time shouldn't be long but it shouldn't be too fast either, because you want these objects to appear approachable. Objects that are moving fast aren't as approachable as slower-moving objects. Five seconds is a good amount of time for the animation, so set the frame count to 150 frames. Making the object spin is easy because of the rotation tool. Again, going off of the idea that you don't want the objects to spin rapidly, one complete spin every five seconds will look good on these coins, as shown in Figure 10-25.

Follow these steps:

1. **Go to frame 0.**

2. **Insert a keyframe.**

3. **Go to frame 150.**

4. **Change the Z rotation to 360.**

5. **Insert a keyframe.**

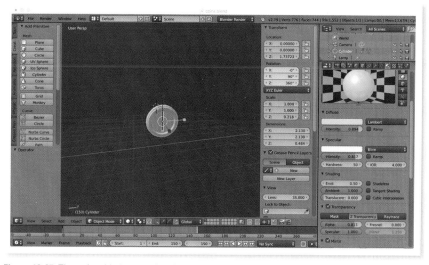

Figure 10-25: The coin with the completed rotation.

This will cause the coins to spin in place. Most of the changes to the coin are purely for visual reasons. You want the coin to stand out so that the player knows to pick it up. One other thing that you can do to make it stand out is have it float up and down along the z-axis. That way the players will be able to see the coin bouncing in place instead of moving around like the enemy grunt or crashing down like the crusher. Slow, simple animations, like the one shown in Figure 10-26, are the best.

1. In frame 0, change the Z position to 2.

2. Insert a keyframe.

3. Go to frame 40.

4. Change the Z position to 1.

5. Insert a keyframe.

6. Go to frame 80.

7. Change the Z position to 2.5.

8. Insert a keyframe.

9. Go to frame 115.

10. Change the Z position to 1.

11. Insert a keyframe.

12. Go to frame 150.

13. Change the Z position to 2.

14. Insert a keyframe.

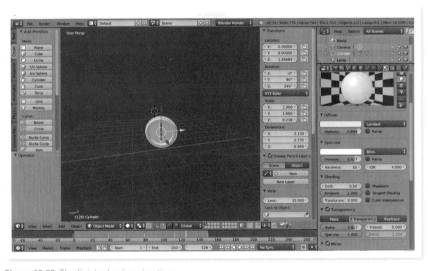

Figure 10-26: The finished coin animation.

CHAPTER

11

Coloring and Lighting
Your Game Level

This chapter is about setting up the level by adjusting the small things, such as the ground color and the background, as well as the lighting. In this chapter, I'll explain how to change the ground material so that it stands out from the background, how to change the ambient lighting from the environment, and how to set up the lighting in the game.

You'll also learn about how lighting changes a game and how to properly light a game so that the shapes are clearly distinguished in 3D. I'll explain how three-point lighting setups work and the difference between the different lights you can create in Unity.

CHANGING THE GROUND COLOR

When you design your levels, think about how you can separate your level from the background. This may seem like an obvious bit of advice, but many game developers fall into the trap of not distinguishing which parts of the level can be interacted with and which parts are just a part of the background. In your platformer, this isn't as much of an issue because the background and level don't really mix, but you should get into the habit of distinguishing the background from the parts of your level that players can interact with. Indicating clearly what parts of the environment are able to be hopped on or grabbed can help prevent player frustration, which is the major balance that you have to strike when developing your game.

As of right now, the game has very little color in it (see Figure 11-1). The level is just white on a gray-blue background, with the only sprinklings of color coming from the characters and pickup items. The level is visually dull. This problem will be partially fixed when you import the characters you made in Chapter 10, but right now the level needs to pop a little more from the background to separate it and give the game some much-needed color.

REMEMBER

Frustration is okay when you *intend* the player to get frustrated. Hard levels can lead to a positive frustration because they encourage the player to continue playing to conquer the level, but you have to understand that there is a difference between frustration that's a result of difficulty and frustration that comes from poor design. Dark Souls is frustrating on purpose, and it's designed to be difficult. Sonic the Hedgehog (Sonic '06) has glitches and poor design choices that make it frustrating. Try to control what the player is feeling in particular levels; if you don't design carefully, player enjoyment might take a hit.

Follow these steps:

1. **Create a new material and name it Ground.**

   You'll be using the new material as the main color for the ground and editing it so that it gives a nice pop to the level itself. Creating one material specifically for the ground can help you when you need to adjust the color at different points because all the objects assigned with that material will change.

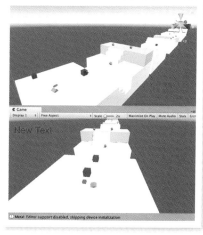

Figure 11-1: The game right now.

2. **Change the Diffuse Color of ground to a darker color.**

   This will make assigning the color to all the objects easier because you'll easily be able to tell which objects have been assigned the color and which ones haven't.

3. **Assign the color from Step 2 to all the platform objects (the ground of the level; see Figure 11-2 for an example).**

   Don't assign the color to the stairs or the respawn areas yet. There's a faster way to change the color of all the stairs, and you want to have the respawn points stick out from the new color. The new color will be similar to the respawn color anyway, so altering it won't be necessary.

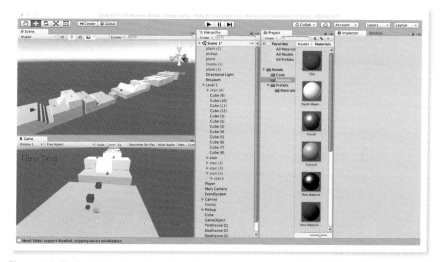

Figure 11-2: The level with the color assigned.

4. **Assign the color from Step 2 to the stairs.**

   Just assign the color to one staircase. Then you can select the whole stairs prefab and click Apply near the top to assign the color across all the staircases (see Figure 11-3).

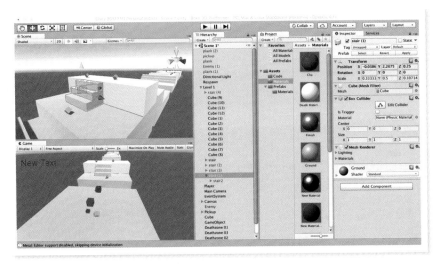

Figure 11-3: Applying the color to the stairs.

5. **Change the Diffuse Color to a deep green color.**

6. **Change the Metallic Color to 0.**

   This will prevent the material from looking metallic and having the specular tint of a metallic object.

7. **Change the Smoothness to 0.**

   Smoothness controls the specular of the object and makes it smoother and crisper or blurry along the edge. For this ground, keep the smoothness 0.

8. **Make sure Emission is off.**

   Emission controls whether the object has its own personal glow so it's less affected by the lights in the scene, or not.

Figure 11-4: The ground color Inspector.

See Figure 11-4 for an example of what the Inspector should look like.

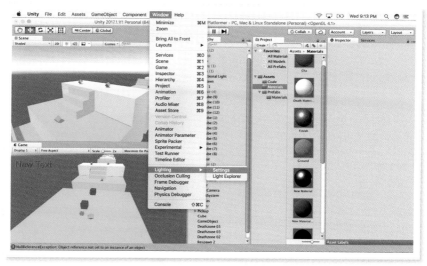

Figure 11-5: Accessing the lighting settings.

EDITING THE ENVIRONMENTAL LIGHTING

Now that the level's ground has been set up and is a nice color that complements the game's already cartoony theme, it's time to learn a bit more about the environmental lighting of the game. Environmental lighting controls the natural lighting that is affected by the environment. Think of it as a tint to the scene that highlights the different parts of the scene but also matches the coloring of the environment.

To access the lighting settings, choose Window ⇨ Lighting ⇨ Settings (see Figure 11-5). A window appears showing the different lighting options you have in Unity, but for the sake of this project you'll only need to worry about the Environment section of the window (see Figure 11-6).

You control the individual lights in the Inspector window in Unity, but the lighting settings window helps you control the various settings for the scene's lighting. The environment settings can help you give the scene's lighting a tint to help make the scene more lively and give the environment a different feeling.

A red tint to the scene can give the game a warmer feeling, making things

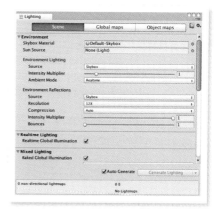

Figure 11-6: The lighting settings.

seem hot or feel as if the sun is setting within the game. A blue tint gives a cooler feeling, making things seem colder. Colors can help indicate the time or season that the game takes place in, which helps you better create the world for your player. Naturally, the settings base the environmental lightings off the skybox that the scene has — the background of the game.

In order to create a skybox, you would need to create six separate images to cover the bottom, top, left, right, front, and back of the scene. Adjusting the lighting and coloring of the scene will work just as well to help give the environment a nice feeling for the player to be immersed in. Follow these steps:

1. **From the Source drop-down list, choose Gradient.**

   Here's a description of the various options, for your reference:

   - **Skybox:** Bases the colors off the currently set skybox background. In this case, the colors are a light blue that go to a gray color.

   - **Gradient:** Similar to Skybox except you can choose the coloring for the fading in the light. You can choose three colors for the gradient to fade among.

   - **Sky Color:** The top color, this color affects the scene from above, as if there were a light shining directly down onto the objects.

   - **Equator Color:** The mid color, this color effects the objects as if the light were coming from the front and sides of the object.

   - **Ground Color:** The bottom color that affects objects from below.

   - **Color:** Tints the color of the scene all at once with one specific color. This can be useful for quick lighting setups.

2. **Change the sky color to a light blue.**

3. **Change the equator color to purple.**

4. **Change the ground color to green.**

The gradient in Figure 11-7 will change the color setup of the scene to better reflect the more distinctive shapes within the

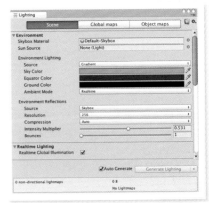

Figure 11-7: The Gradient source.

scene. The light blue will give the top of the shape a nice distinctive bright color to indicate it's the top. The purple will contrast nicely with the light blue, giving the sides of the objects a distinctive difference from the top. Finally, the green won't affect much in the scene, but it will imitate the bouncing of the light off of the ground so that the bottom of the objects are tinted slightly green.

UNDERSTANDING LIGHTING

Lighting is one of the most important parts of game design that is often overlooked. Games can be changed by lighting, even subtly. A game that looks like it takes place in the middle of the day with vibrant colors can be drastically changed with just the angle of the lighting. Right now, the scene looks like Figure 11-8. You're going to be adjusting the direction of the light to help give the scene more vibrancy.

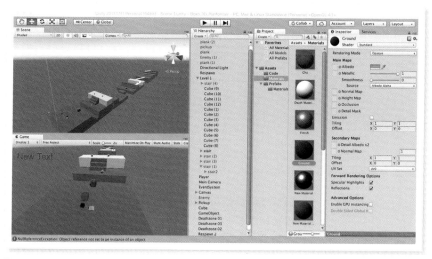

Figure 11-8: The scene colored.

Select Directional Light from the Hierarchy window. The directional light acts as a light source that comes from an indistinct distance away. That means that no matter where it is in the scene, the lighting will remain the same because the directional light just adjusts the angle that the light is coming in. Try rotating the light to better see how the lights change (see Figure 11-9).

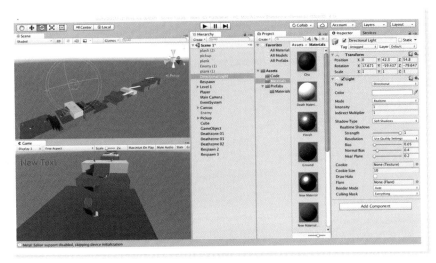

Figure 11-9: Adjusting the angle of the directional light.

There are four types of lights that you can choose from within Unity. To create any of these lights, simply choose GameObject ⇨ Light, and you'll see four different options:

- **Directional lights:** Directional lights light up the scene from a certain angle. They represent a sun or other bright object shining from no specific distance away. In this game, these will be the lights you'll use to create a three-point lighting setup.

- **Point lights:** Point lights light up a certain point in the scene. They're like a small orb of light that lights up a particular spot in the scene.

- **Spot lights:** Spot lights are the combination of point lights and directional lights. They're a light pointing in a specific direction that comes from a specific spot in the scene. They light up an area within a cone of light. These lights are particularly good at creating flashlights.

- **Area lights:** Area lights light up an entire area of the scene. They're much larger than point lights and light up the entire area uniformly, as opposed to point lights, which fade out near the edges.

Different lighting setups can change entire games. Imagine horror if games like Slender: The Arrival or Resident Evil took place in the daylight. Lighting is part of what builds an environment or feeling in a game. Imagine if you were to attach a point light to the player character, and the only light source they had was this one light (see Figure 11-10). The game would be totally different and probably less fun. It would no longer be a platformer game but an exploration game, with the player having to navigate around the scene with very limited information.

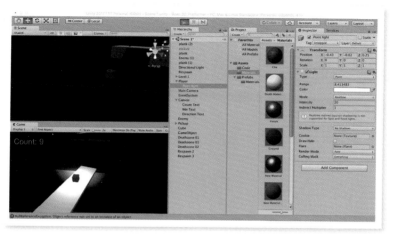

Figure 11-10: The scene lit by only a point light.

In film and animation, there is a technique used by filmmakers that help create a complete three-dimensional view of a character and environment. Three-point lighting is used to help visually show the character in 3D while softening some of the darker shadows on the character and separating them from the background. This is done with three lights:

- **Key light:** The brightest light in the scene, the key light's goal is to highlight the subject of the scene to show the audience the character's face or light up the object of the scene. This is the primary light. It's usually pointed at one side of the character or the subject of the scene.

- **Fill light:** The fill light is pointed at the other (front) side of the character to help fill in the dark shadows created by the key light. It isn't as bright as the key light because its job is to lessen the shadows instead of drown them out.

- **Back light:** The purpose of the back light is to separate the character from the background. Generally speaking, the purpose of this light is to prevent the character from being seen as part of the background by creating a small halo around the character to help distinguish them from the rest of the game.

In your game, you'll set up a simple three-point lighting setup to light up your scene properly and give some nice shadows to your game and help distinguish its 3D objects:

1. **Duplicate your directional light two times (for a total of three).**

2. **Direct each light in a different direction toward the player character — two pointing from the camera down toward the player and one pointing up from behind the player.**

3. **Select one light (near the camera) to be your key light.**

   In the Inspector, when you select the key light, you'll see a
   Light component. Change the color to White. Change the intensity
   to 0.8 (1 is slightly bright and causes the scene to be slightly
   overexposed, with too much light). Change the strength of the
   real-time shadows to 0.15 to prevent the harsh shadows that you
   have right now.

4. **Select the other light near the camera and have that light be the fill
   light.**

   In the Inspector, change the color to also be a slightly darker shade
   of white. Change the intensity to 0.4. Make sure the strength of the
   real-time shadows is 0.

5. **Select the final light that's behind the player — that's your back
   light.**

   Change the color to a light gray. Change the intensity to 0.2. Make
   sure the strength of the real-time shadows is 0.

When you finish, your scene should look similar to Figure 11-11.

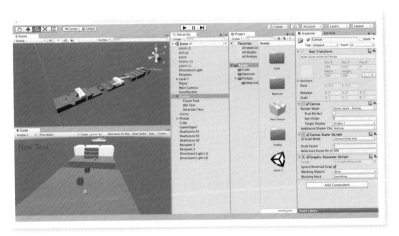

Figure 11-11: The scene properly lit.

CREATING FOG

Another way to help bring the scene more to life is to add fog to the
scene. Fog, as the name suggests, disrupts the visibility of the scene and
makes objects further away from the camera blurrier and faded. Fog has
been used in games for years to help with processing power as well as to

give a sense of mystery or distance within the game. When you look off to the horizon, shapes become faded the further away from you they are.

In games, you can simulate this effect using fog. First, you'll have to go back to the lighting settings window that you used earlier to change the environmental lighting.

1. **To create fog, scroll down in the lighting settings to the Other Settings tab.**

2. **Check the box next to Fog in the drop-down.**

   This will create a fog for the game. The closer the camera is, the less fog there is in the scene.

3. **Change the color of the fog to a grayish green to match the coloring in the game already set.**

4. **Make sure the Mode is exponential squared.**

5. **Keep the Density at 0.01.**

This will create a nice fog in the game window so that when you play the game, the fog will appear on the horizon of the game, obscuring the player's ability to see beyond a certain point clearly. This will create a sense of distance in the game's world and give overall more life to the game's setting. As you can see in Figure 11-12, the fog helps shape the 3D nature of the level and create a nice view for the player.

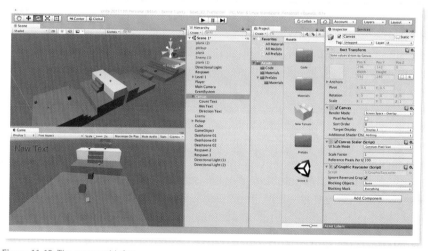

Figure 11-12: The scene with fog.

In gaming, fog acts as a way to limit the player's ability to see farther ahead in the level. In some games, fog is used to add tension to the scene by limiting the player's ability to plan ahead; in other games, fog acts as a way to help ease the need to render entire levels at once (which can be difficult, especially for older consoles). In this case, the fog is more of an aesthetic choice.

Now before you add characters and objects in Chapter 12, take a moment to compare the images at the end of the chapter to the images at the beginning of the chapter. Already, you can see how lighting and color have brought more life to the scene than was previously there. The game is hitting its final preparations!

Importing Your Characters into Your Game

In this chapter, you'll import your characters and objects into Unity to finish setting up your game. This chapter is the culmination of all the previous chapters in this book. You'll combine what you've worked on in Blender and Unity into one final version of the game, with very little coding left to do.

Here, you'll learn how to import the characters and animations into Unity and set up the animations so that they begin to play when you start the game. You'll also learn how to set up animation controls for your main player character so that the animations only play when the corresponding controls are used in the game. The goal of this chapter is to have the finished version of the game that will only require a little bit of alteration and fixing up in the next chapter.

FIXING YOUR PLAYER CHARACTER FOR IMPORTING INTO UNITY

You'll be able to import most of the animations that you made in Chapter 10 with no problem. But Unity doesn't like every type of animation — namely, shape keys. Unity was built to import a variation of shape keys, called blend shapes, that are used within programs like Maya. Luckily there are plenty of workarounds for this problem, but none of these workarounds is within Unity itself, so that means you must dive back into Blender one last time to export the file into a version that Unity can read and use.

Open your character in Blender (see Figure 12-1). You won't actually be able to see the changes that you have to make to the character on the screen right now because it involves something called a *dope sheet*. In hand-drawn animations, dope sheets were outlines for animators to use so that they could determine when a specific animation would happen and for how long. It was a simple outline for the animators to work from. In Blender, the dope sheet gives you the ability to adjust the animation timing and order. You can use it to move key frames around to either speed up or slow down certain animations.

To open the dope sheet, go to the lower-left corner of the Timeline and find the small clock icon that looks like a drop-down menu. Click that clock and then click the Dope Sheet icon with three dots (two gray, one orange). This will turn your Timeline into a dope sheet.

Figure 12-1: Your character in Blender.

TIP

You can actually do this with *any* of the different windows in Blender. If you look at the lower-left corner of any of the window sections, you'll notice a similar drop-down menu. This goes with Blender's ability to be customized to best fit your needs. I just prefer to switch the dope sheet, shown in Figure 12-2, with the Timeline because both have similar functions and, most of the time, when I use the dope sheet, I need the other windows.

When you've opened up the dope sheet, you'll see a menu bar at the bottom. Next to that menu bar, you'll see the Key drop-down. Select Shape Key Editor from the Key drop-down menu.

Now what you're doing is making the shape key animation so that it's being read as a location-based animation (something that Unity has no issues reading). To do this, select all the frames:

1. **Hold Shift and select each frame individually.**

2. **Press B (for bounding box) and drag across the Timeline to select all the frames.**

3. **Press A (for all) while hovering your mouse over the dope sheet to select them all.**

Figure 12-2: The dope sheet.

When you've done this, at the bottom of the dope sheet, next to where it says KeyAction, click the button that has an F. This saves the data block even when it has no users. For the sake of simplicity, this will give you the ability to import your shape key animations into Unity without any problems.

Now change the Shape Key Editor to Action Editor. This will open up the actions of the animation (the key frame changes to the location, rotation, and scale, as shown in Figure 12-3). At frames 0 and 245 insert a key frame using the animation tab in the 3D view window, and select

Figure 12-3: The Action Editor.

location when Unity prompts you what this key frame will be affecting. This will create a range for Unity to read the file in.

After you finish, save your file. Then choose File ⇨ Export ⇨ FBX (.fbx), as shown in Figure 12-4, and save the file into your Blender folder that the other files are saved in. This will save your work so that Unity will be able to read it with little problems. Exit Blender now and open up Unity.

Figure 12-4: Saving the file as an FBX file.

IMPORTING YOUR PLAYER CHARACTER INTO UNITY

Now it's time to import your first character into Blender. To do this, follow these steps:

1. **Open Unity and go to the Prefabs folder in the Project window.**

2. **Open the Finder window on a Mac or Windows Explorer on a PC.**

3. **Drag the FBX file from the Blender folder directly into the Prefabs folder.**

   This will create a prefab of your character. In the drop-down of the character's prefab are all the different components of your character.

4. **Drag the prefab onto the screen to make the new character.**

The first thing you'll notice in Figure 12-5 is how large the character is compared to the rest of the scene. This is because Unity's units are half the size of Blender's units.

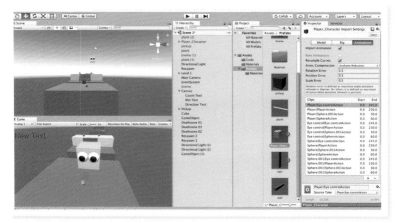

Figure 12-5: The player character in the scene.

5. **To fix this import error, select the prefab of the player character that you just created.**

   In the Inspector window, you'll notice that the window has changed to Import Setting. When you import an animation or external 3D object, the window will open the Import Settings when you select the prefab. You'll go further into the Rig and Animation tabs later in this chapter.

6. **Click the Model tab.**

   You'll see many different settings that can be checked or changed.

7. **Change the Scale Factor to 0.5.**

8. **Make sure the following boxes are all checked:**

   - Use File Scale

   - Read/Write Enables

   - Import BlendShapes

   - Generate Colliders

   - Weld Vertices

   - Import Visibility

9. **Go down to the Materials section in the model tab, and make sure Import Materials is checked.**

10. **Change the Material Naming drop-down to Model Name + Model's Matter.**

    This will prevent multiple files from changing the materials to match other materials with similar names.

SETTING UP THE CHARACTER

Because of the animations you've made, when the player character begins, it will automatically move to point (0,0,0). The way Unity reads the animations causes the characters or objects to reset to where the characters or objects move in relation to the center point of Unity. The simplest way to fix this problem is to give the animation a new center point for it to be based on. This is done via parenting.

These next steps are mainly to help you practice creating and placing an object for the character and parenting the character to them. To save time, you can just parent the player character to your practice character and turn off the mesh render for that practice character. This will have the same effect as doing it in the following way, but if you feel like practicing, these steps are useful:

1. Delete the previous character cube.

2. Create a new cube.

Figure 12-6: Parenting the cube.

3. In the Hierarchy, drag the player character into the cube to parent it to the cube, as shown in Figure 12-6.

4. In the cube's Inspector, turn Mesh Render off.

   This will make it so that the cube won't render in the game and won't be visible in the game, despite it still affecting the game itself.

5. Change the name of the cube to Character Controller.

6. **Position the cube to be in a location at the beginning of the level.**

7. **Apply the char script to the cube (see Figure 12-7).**

8. **Reapply all the targets so that they match what they were in your original character (see Figure 12-8).**

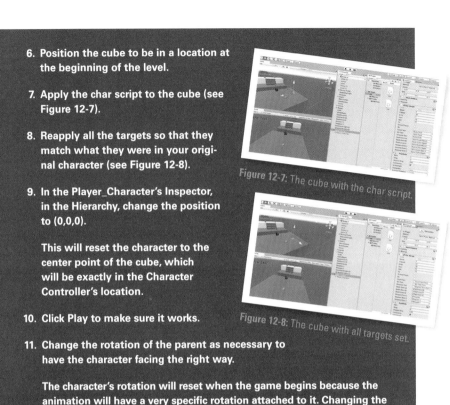

Figure 12-7: The cube with the char script.

9. **In the Player_Character's Inspector, in the Hierarchy, change the position to (0,0,0).**

   This will reset the character to the center point of the cube, which will be exactly in the Character Controller's location.

10. **Click Play to make sure it works.**

Figure 12-8: The cube with all targets set.

11. **Change the rotation of the parent as necessary to have the character facing the right way.**

   The character's rotation will reset when the game begins because the animation will have a very specific rotation attached to it. Changing the rotation of the parent will change the direction that the character is facing.

SETTING UP THE ANIMATION

Now you'll notice that either the animation will only play once and not again or it won't play at all when you click the Play button to play the game. This is because you still have yet to set up the animation for the character. This will require you to use the Rig and Animation tabs of the Inspector window of the prefab.

1. **Open up the Rig tab in the inspector window.**

   There are four animation types to choose from in the drop-down:

   • **None:** When you aren't importing an animation.

   • **Legacy:** The older way to import animations. This method doesn't work properly with an animation controller, so it's not good for using for the player character.

- **Generic:** The basic import method that imports the animations while keeping the code in a way that Unity can read and alter as necessary.

- **Humanoid:** Imports humanoid characters that have rigging, attaching bones or armatures to the mesh so that different parts can bend.

2. **For this project, choose the Generic type.**

3. **Change the Avatar Definition to Create for This Model.**

4. **Change the Root Node to None.**

5. **Click the Animations tab (see Figure 12-9).**

6. **Scroll down to the Clips section.**

   You see a ton of options and break-downs. These are just the different animation parts within the animation that Unity can recognize. Sometimes this is accurate but most of the time, I find it's more reliable to just do it yourself.

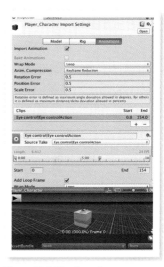

7. **Delete all the options and breakdowns by selecting them and clicking the minus sign (–) in the right corner.**

8. **Click the plus sign (+) once.**

   Figure 12-9: The first clip you create.

9. **For the Source Take drop-down menu, choose Eye control|Eye controlAction.**

10. **For this first animation, change the name of the clip to Idle.**

    The blue highlights on the Timeline indicate the part of the animation that the clip is using.

11. **Adjust the Timeline to include only the Idle animation of the character.**

    My animation starts at 0 and ends at 154.

12. **Follow steps 8 through 11 for the walk and jump animations, naming them Walking and Jump, respectively, as shown in Figure 12-10.**

After you finish setting up the animations, you have to make sure that your character is accessing them properly:

Figure 12-10: The first clip you create.

1. **Select your character on the Hierarchy and look into the Inspector.**

   You'll notice that there will be an animation component added to your character. You'll see an animation part with a place to put an animation clip.

2. **Select the little circle next to the none (Animation Clip).**

   The select AnimationClip window (shown in Figure 12-11) appears.

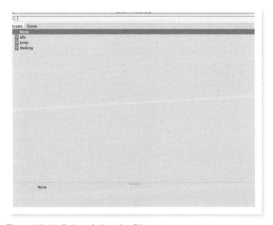

Figure 12-11: Select AnimationClip

The clip that you choose will be the base animation for your character (the animation that the character will start the game in).

3. **Select the Idle clip and double-click the Idle clip.**

   This will set your Idle animation as the starting animation for your game.

4. **From the Animations drop-down, select Size.**

   You'll see a number of elements below it matching the size.

5. **For your animation, you only need three elements so change the size to 3.**

6. **Make sure that the elements that you do have are the Idle, Walking, and Jump elements.**

   If they aren't, change them.

REMEMBER
Save your project and scene.

CREATING THE ANIMATION CONTROLLER FOR YOUR CHARACTER

The character now has the animation set up to work, but when you click Play nothing happens. This is because there is nothing telling the game that the animation should be playing. In other words, there is nothing controlling the animation.

To control the animation so that the proper animations play when the character is moving, you need an animator controller. An animator controller tells the character how the animations interact with one another.

To create an animator controller, like the one shown in Figure 12-12, right-click in the Project window. You can create the animator controller in any folder, but for the sake of simplicity I prefer creating the controller in either the prefabs folder or directly in the assets folder. Choose Create ⇨ Animator Controller. A new animator controller will be created. Rename it to Character_animator. Double-clicking this new controller will open a new tab on the Scene window called Animator.

After you open the controller window, you'll realize that it's empty, except for two boxes: Any State and Entry. To fix this, open your Player character prefab and scroll down. At the bottom of the prefab, you'll see three tabs for the three

Figure 12-12: Creating an animator controller.

REMEMBER
You'll still be able to access the Scene window simply by clicking it in the upper-left corner. Double-clicking the animator will only open a new tab, not close the Scene window.

clips you have for the different animations for the character. Drag all three of them into the Animator window. Three new boxes will appear, one for each of the different clips (see Figure 12-13).

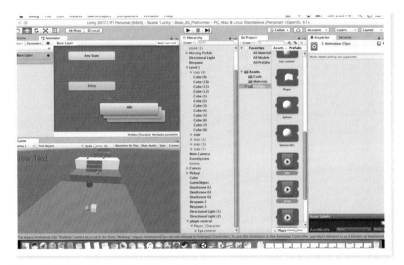

Figure 12-13: The different clips in the animator.

You'll also notice that there is now an orange arrow pointing from Entry to Idle. This indicates that in the animator's view, the Idle animation is the primary animation for the character, which is useful because for your game this is the case.

If the Idle animation is not highlighted orange with an orange arrow pointing to it, or if you want a different animation as the primary animation for the game, right-click Entry and select Set StateMachine Default State. Then select the desired default, and you'll see the orange arrow move to that one and change its color to orange.

After you create these new boxes for each of the animations, move them apart from each other so that you can clearly read each of them and there is some space in between them all. Make sure that the default state (currently Idle) is the one that is closest to Entry and Any State, with the other two below or to the side of Idle, with Idle between them (see Figure 12-14). This will do nothing to the game itself but will make it easier visually to navigate.

Now you have to determine how each of these states relates to each other:

1. **Right-click Any State and choose Make Transition.**

2. **Select Idle After.**

   An arrow should now point from Any State to Idle.

3. **Right-click Idle and choose Make Transition.**

4. **Select Jump.**

   This will make it so that the character can transition from the Idle animation to the Jump animation.

5. **Repeat Steps 3 and 4 for Walking instead of Jump.**

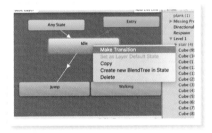

Figure 12-14: Creating the transitions.

After you create all these transitions (see Figure 12-14), you also need to make it so that the character can transition back from Walking and Jump to Idle, as well as from Walking to Jump and vice versa. Create transitions as you did in the steps earlier, but instead of doing it from Idle, do it from Walking and Jump to Idle and to each other.

This will create the transitions, so the animator knows how each of the animations relate to each other, but there is still nothing to indicate when these animations happen. As of right now, the only animation that will play is the Idle animation. You need to create triggers, as in Figure 12-15, to indicate when the controller will work.

In the Animator window, click the Parameters tab. On the Parameters tab, you'll see List Is Empty, indicating there is nothing that is affecting the animations just yet. Click the plus sign (+) and select Trigger. This will create a trigger for the animations to be affected by. Name this trigger Jump and then create another one named Walk.

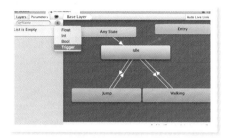

Figure 12-15: Creating the trigger.

After you create these triggers, you have to indicate when they're used (see Figure 12-16):

1. **Select one of the arrows leading to Jump.**

   In the Inspector window, you see Transitions and Conditions. In Conditions, it says *non-* with a drop-down menu.

2. **From the Non- drop-down menu, select Jump.**

3. **Repeat steps 1 and 2 for all the arrows leading to Jump.**

4. **Repeat steps 1 and 2 for all the arrows leading to Walking.**

5. **Substitute Jump for Walk.**

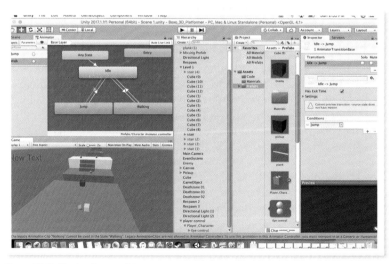

Figure 12-16: Setting the conditions.

This will make it so that you can transition from the idle pose to the jump and walk poses easily. The problem is that there is no way to transition from those poses back to idle. So, create a third trigger named Idle and repeat the steps to link the idle to the other poses.

TIP

In the Inspector above the conditions, you'll also see settings with a time-line, and above it is Has Exit Time. This means that the animation will finish before going into the new animation when it's triggered. Although this can be useful for some cases, you want to uncheck it so that it doesn't interfere with the animation of the game.

CODING THE CONTROLLER

It always comes back to coding in computers and gaming. Now that you've created the controller and the character, you have to link the two so that the character's animations can be properly controlled by the animator controller and the animator controller can be linked to certain button presses on the keyboard. The code for the controller is actually super simple compared to some of the codes from earlier chapters.

Before you begin coding, you have to link the controller to the player character. To do this, select the player character on the Hierarchy and in the Inspector select Add Component. In the Miscellaneous menu, you'll find an Animator component. After you add the component, inside the component you'll see a controller target. Select the circle next to it, and select the animator that you just finished creating. This will link the controller to the character.

After you link the controller with the character, go into the code folder in the assets and create a new code named Animat. This will act as the animation code for your player character. Attach it to the player character, and open up the code.

You'll open a blank code. Delete all the grayed-out comments and change `void Update` to `void FixedUpdate`. This will set up the code for what you need to control the character's animations. Then follow these steps:

1. **Above** `void Start ()`, **add** `Animator anim;`.

   This will indicate the type of code that `anim` is. This tells the code that `anim` controls an animator and will affect it directly.

2. **Inside** `void Start ()` **add** `anim = GetComponent <Animator> ();`.

   This tells the code that when the code begins the `anim` will access the specific component within the object that is an Animator. In this case, the animator is the `player_controller` that you made earlier.

   Let's say you wanted to make multiple characters that move at once. Instead of needing different codes for each of them, this code can work for all of them because it doesn't specify a specific animator. Instead, it just goes off of the component.

3. **Inside** `FixedUpdate`, **you'll add several** `if` **statements:**

   ```
   if (Input.GetKeyDown (KeyCode.Space)) { anim.
     SetTrigger ("Jump"); }
   ```

   This will make it so that if the spacebar is pressed, the code will send a message to the animator to activate the Jump trigger. This will cause the jump animation to play.

   ```
   if (Input.GetKeyDown (KeyCode.W)) { anim.SetTrigger
     ("Walk"); }
   ```

   This will make it so that when the W key is pressed, the character's walk trigger will activate, causing the walk animation to begin. Repeat this code three more times for the different movement keys (A, S, and D) in place of W.

   ```
   if (Input.anyKey == false) { anim.SetTrigger
     ("Idle"); }
   ```

   This code is the odd code in the bunch. Although the other codes trigger when a specific button is clicked, this code only activates when no button is being clicked. When nothing is being touched, the Idle trigger activates putting the character into the Idle animation.

Figure 12-17: The finished code.

After you finish the coding (see Figure 12-17), go into the prefab for player character and go into the Inspector. Click the Animation tab and make sure that all of the clips have Loop Time checked so that the player will continuously repeat the motion as long as the key is held.

Save your project and then test the animation by playing the game. The code should cause the characters to move and animate on the key presses. If they don't, check back through the codes to see if you missed anything.

REMEMBER

Save your project and scene.

IMPORTING THE OTHER CHARACTERS AND OBJECTS

The player character is easily the hardest character to import into Unity. The rest of the characters are fairly straightforward because they don't use shape keys or need a controller for their animations. First up: the enemy grunt.

IMPORTING THE ENEMY GRUNT

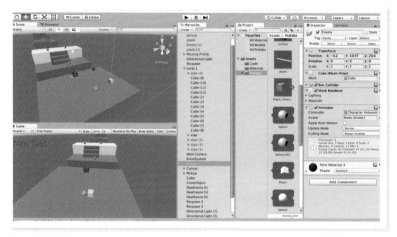

Figure 12-18: The enemy grunt.

To import the enemy grunt (see Figure 12-18), follow these steps:

1. **Delete the enemy grunt stand-ins that you already made, and replace them with empties in their spots.**

Name the empties differently so that you can keep track of which empty is which. Enemy Grunt is a good name for the empties. Just add a number or letter at the end so that you can tell which empty is which.

2. **Using the Finder (Mac) or Windows Explorer (PC), drag the enemy. blend file into Unity's prefab folder.**

3. **Select the prefab, and in the Inspector, change the Scale Factor to 0.5.**

4. **Make sure the following tabs are all checked:**

   - Use File Scale

   - Read/Write Enables

- Import BlendShapes

- Generate Colliders

- Weld Vertices

- Import Visibility

5. **From the Material Naming drop-down, select Model Name + Model's Matter.**

6. **Click the Rig tab.**

7. **Change the Rig to Legacy.**

   You aren't using a controller for this character.
   I find that Legacy import is actually more stable and easier to use for importing the enemy characters and objects.

8. **Click the Animation tab.**

9. **Make sure that the Wrap Mode is set to Loop.**

   In Generic, it's Loop Time; in Legacy, it's a Wrap Mode.

10. **Drag and drop two enemy grunts into the Scene window.**

These steps are actually identical to the steps used to import the player character in the beginning of the chapter. Steps 2 through 5 will be used in every import.

If the eye cylinder is not attached to the box, just select it in the Enemy drop-down in the Hierarchy and move it so that it's inside the enemy.

11. **Parent each of the grunts to one of the empties created in Step 1.**

12. **Set the position of the empties to (0,0,0).**

   This will place them in the direct middle of the empty.

   Think back to the player controller cube that you created earlier. This is because the character will move around the (0,0,0) point. The same rule applies for all the animations that you'll be importing in. The difference is that, because you want the collider to be on the enemy character and not the center point, you'll want to use an empty instead of a box.

13. **Moving the empty that the enemy grunt is in, make sure the grunt is just touching the ground (as in Figure 12-19).**

14. **Select the enemy in the Hierarchy.**

15. **In the Inspector, make sure on the Animation tab that Play Automatically is clicked.**

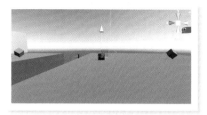

Figure 12-19: The enemy grunt in position.

16. **Choose Add a Component ⟶ Physics ⟶ Box Collider.**

17. **On the Box Collider tab, make sure Is Trigger is clicked.**

    This will make it so that the character will be affected by the box collider.

REMEMBER

Save your project and scene.

18. **Change the Tag at the top to Enemy.**

19. **Repeat steps 12 through 18 for the second enemy grunt (see Figure 12-20).**

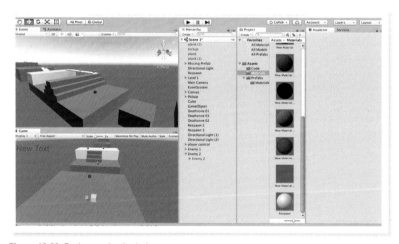

Figure 12-20: Both enemies in their proper spots.

IMPORTING THE CRUSHER

The crusher is slightly more complicated than the enemy grunt because it actually requires two colliders to work properly. One of those colliders has to kill the player while the player only has to be able to jump on the other one.

First, import in the Crusher using steps 2 through 5 from the "Importing the enemy grunt" section. Delete the stand-in hazard and replace it with the empty and name it Crusher (center the empty on the *x*-axis). Follow these steps:

1. **On the Rig tab, change the rig to Legacy.**

2. **On the Animation tab, change the Wrap Mode to Loop.**

3. **Drag the crusher into the scene and parent it to the empty created.**

    You'll notice that the crusher has something parented to it. This is because in Blender the upper section and the lower section of the crusher were two different objects. The upper section was parented to the bottom section, and that parenting carries over into Unity.

4. **Set the position to (0,0,0).**

5. **Adjust the empty so that the crusher's bottom is just touching the level.**

6. **Select the crusher on the Hierarchy, and make sure that the animator has Play Automatically checked.**

7. **Choose Add a Component ➪ Physics ➪ Box Collider.**

8. **Do not make this collider a trigger, and do not add a tag.**

    This will make the bottom of the crusher a platform that the player can go on.

9. **Open the Crusher parent, and select the child inside of it (the top part of the crusher).**

10. **Choose Add a Component ➪ Physics ➪ Box Collider.**

11. **Make the collider a trigger.**

12. **Change the tag at the top to enviroHazard 3.**

After you do so, you'll have a completed crusher like the one shown in Figure 12-21.

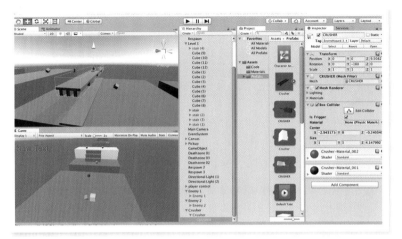

Figure 12-21: The crusher.

This will make it so that the crusher's top part will act as the environmental hazard stand-in did, while the bottom part will act as a platform that the players can jump on. If you want to have two separate colliders on an object, you can do so by adding a new collider in through adding a component, but if you want it so that each collider does something different, the object needs to have two separate parts.

IMPORTING THE COINS

As before, the coins need to imported using steps 2 through 5 from the "Importing the enemy grunt" section. Unlike before, because there are so many pickup items, it's easier to delete all the pickup items and create one empty near the beginning. Name this empty `coin_pickup`. Following the steps from earlier, make sure that the rig of the coin is Legacy and that its wrap is Loop.

Drag the coin into the scene and parent it to `coin_pickup`. Then set its position to (0,0,0) so that the coin is centered on the empty. Make sure that its animation component has Play Automatically clicked and that it has the pickup tag. Also, add a mesh collider to the coins instead of a box collider because the shape is a cylinder and not a box. Make sure that both Convex and IsTrigger are checked.

Then drag the `coin_pickup` into the prefabs menu so that it's a prefab. Using the `coin_pickup` prefab, place the coins throughout the level in similar spots to the pickup stand-ins from earlier.

TIP

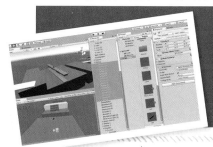

When placing the coins, keep in mind that the coin is floating above the center point, so you should place the coins closer to the ground so that the coin appears to be bouncing up and down from the ground (see Figure 12-22).

Figure 12-22: The coins placed.

TIP

The bridges will be replaced by a moving platform next, so place coins with the moving platform in mind in those sections.

At the end of the level where the end goal prefab was, place another coin, but change the size of the empty on this one coin to X = 3, Y = 3, and Z = 3 so that it's three times the size of the other coins and looks like Figure 12-23. This coin will act as the end goal to the level, and its size will help indicate its importance above the other coins. Go into the coin's Inspector and change the tag from pickup to final to make sure that when the player runs into it, they're given the win condition.

Figure 12-23: The end coin.

IMPORTING THE MOVING PLATFORM

The last thing to add into the game is a moving platform (see Figure 12-24). Following the same steps as earlier, delete all the bridges and replace them with empties. Parent a moving platform to each of the empties so that they're floating in spots that used to be covered by the bridges. The only major difference in the steps for this part and the other three is that the box collider that is added to the moving platform should not have Is Trigger checked. When Is Trigger is checked, the character falls through the mesh instead of landing on top of it. Also, the moving platform does not need a tag.

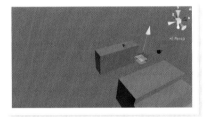

Figure 12-24: The moving platform.

With that, the level is finished and ready to play! Play the game and see what has to be adjusted or fixed. You've finished your first designed and playable level!

13

Play Testing (Again)

This chapter acts as the final cleanup for your level. Like the previous play-testing chapter (Chapter 6), the emphasis of this chapter is on looking back at the aspects of the game that do and don't work, as well as fixing the problems that are within your game. In this chapter, you won't be learning anything new. Instead, you'll refine the aspects of your game that may not work as well as some of the others and ask yourself the questions that will be useful when you aim to set your games apart from other games.

The goal of this chapter is to come out with a completed level that you'll be able to play. This chapter forces you to look back on your game and think about what you do and don't understand about it. In the end, you'll see the benefit of play testing more than once.

TESTING THE SECOND TIME

REMEMBER

For this round of play testing, try to find players that have and haven't played your game before. The play testers you used earlier will know more about the game and can look deeper into some of the problems they may not have noticed earlier or be able to better explain some of the problems that they had with the game earlier. The players who haven't played the game before come in with fresh eyes. They'll help you make sure that the new controls to the game are easy to learn.

You should conduct play testing often in order to create a better game. Game development is about fixing and adjusting things so they work better, so play testing is important at all times, even when you've already done it.

This time, you'll focus on other aspects of your game than what you were focusing on before. When you were looking at your game earlier, you were focusing on the core aspects of the game, what did and didn't make sense, and what could be clearer. This time you're focusing on the parts of your game that need more polish or need to be fixed because they broke with the addition of different parts of the game.

With new play tests come new questions that have to be answered. On top of the questions you asked in the previous play testing, you have new questions that should be answered. These questions range from some simple problems within the game code to creating entirely new assets. Again these questions are asked in no particular order, but all of them should be considered in this new round of play testing.

Ask these questions on your second round of play testing:

- **What has broken in the game? Why?** This question is probably the most obvious question when play testing — whether you're doing it early in the game development or later on. Sometimes aspects of the game are working fine until a new factor comes in and ruins it all. When you play test your game, keep an eye out for some of these problems.

> Never assume that if something was working before, it will continue to work. Game codes are a delicate balancing act. Any small change can break the code, and sometimes these breaks are so small that you may not notice them at first. Identifying these breaks is what play testing is for.

- **Is the game hard or frustrating?** At this point in the development, you should have a pretty good grasp on what works and what doesn't work in your game as it is. This question helps you understand if the "harder" parts of your game are having the desired effect on the players. Players should never feel cheated by the game. As soon as that happens, the game developer has made a mistake in the game.

- **What blocks did you find in the game?** Are there parts of the game that force the game to a halt? Are these parts even able to be overcome or are they impossible? Games that are impossible aren't fun. A player never wants to feel like he *can't* win a game. Sometimes these blocks come in the form of tasks that are too challenging, or just a wall that is too high for the player to get across.

- **Was the game too easy?** Games aren't fun if they don't have some sense of accomplishment for finishing them. Although games that are too difficult can discourage players, games that are too easy make the accomplishments that the players achieve less meaningful.

- **Did the game make sense?** Was the players able to understand the game and play it with little to no confusion? Games should not

REMEMBER

When you play test your game, encourage your players to ask these questions and see if they can answer them. The game should speak for itself. Do not explain the game — after all, you won't be there to explain the game to everyone who plays it in the future.

confuse players (unless the point of the game is to be confusing). Games should make sense and have rules that are clear and easy to understand.

FIXING YOUR GAME

When you finish play testing, acknowledge the problems that were addressed and find ways to fix them. I'll cover some of the problems in this section, but your play testers may identify problems that I don't cover here. But using what you've learned in this book, try to figure out ways to address these issues as they come up, and alter your game to answer the questions the play testers come up with. The game is yours to improve on! This book gives you the bare bones — it's up to you to make it your own.

THE WALL-CLIMBING PROBLEM IS BACK

One thing that broke when the game was given characters and animation was the solution to the wall-climbing problem that you fixed earlier. Using raycasting, you made it so that when the player runs into the wall, he's forced back, preventing him from using the wall as something that they could climb up and use (see Figure 13-1).

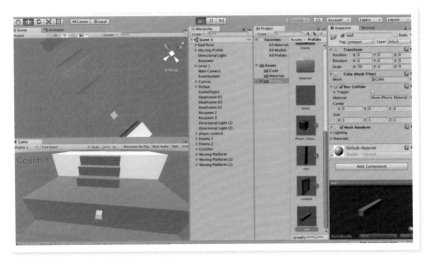

Figure 13-1: Wall climbing.

Checking the character, you see that nothing much has changed. The player is still controlling the character, and the animation is parented to the base player, so although the animation plays, nothing it does actually affects the movement of the character. In the code, nothing is any different. The char code hasn't been changed at all.

The problem isn't with the individual parts but with how they relate to each other. Try running into the staircase from either side and see what happens. One side doesn't change, but when the other side runs into the wall, the character goes backward as if he had the raycast on him. This is because he does.

Raycasting is based on the object's orientation, not the global orientation like the vector directions were. Because of this, the raycast that was on the front of the mesh has been moved to one side of the player. To fix this issue, you just need to change one small aspect of the code, and the player's original movement in the game will be restored.

The `vector3`s that determined the direction of the raycast need to be adjusted to account for this rotation in the mesh. For the example given in Figure 13-2, only the forward direction needed to be changed to left. The down `vector3` didn't need to be changed because the altering of the character's angle did not change the y-axis at all so the down is still in the same place. That's all you need to do. After you finish, save the code and test to make sure that it's working properly.

REMEMBER

Play testing isn't just about fixing the problems; it's about understanding *why* a problem happened in the first place. When something breaks, there is a problem in either the model or the code.

REMEMBER

The animation was facing the wrong direction when you imported it into the game. So to compensate for this you adjusted the angle or rotation of the empty that you attached the character to in Chapter 12. Although this had no effect on the directions that the character moves, it did change the raycasting.

THE COINS ARE GOING DOWN BY TWO EVERY TIME YOU GET HURT IN THE GAME

This problem was a head scratcher. Nothing seemed to change between the variable and the code to affect this change in the game, but every time you run into an enemy or fall off the edge, the character loses two coins as opposed to just one, causing much faster game-overs.

```
83
84    if (Input.GetKey(KeyCode.D))
85    {
86        transform.position += Vector3.right * Time.deltaTime * Speed;
87    }
88
89    if (Input.GetKey (KeyCode.Space) && GroundTouch == true) {
90        transform.position += Vector3.up * Time.deltaTime * jump;
91        if (directionText.text == "Press Space to Jump") {
92            directionText.text = "Left Shift to Sprint";
93        }
94    }
95
96
97    Vector3 gc = transform.TransformDirection (Vector3.down);
98    Vector3 wc = transform.TransformDirection (Vector3.left);
99
100   if (Physics.Raycast (transform.position, gc, 0.5f)) {
101       GroundTouch = true;
102   }
103
104   if (Physics.Raycast (transform.position, wc, 0.4f)) {
105       transform.position += Vector3.back * Time.deltaTime * wall;
106   }
107
108
109 }
110
111 void OnTriggerEnter(Collider other) {
112
113     if (other.gameObject.CompareTag("Pickup"))
114     {
115
116         other.gameObject.SetActive (false);
117         count = count + 1;
118         SetCountText ();
119     }
```

Figure 13-2: Fixing the wall-climbing code.

The problem stems from the game giving back too much information to the code. Although the code isn't on the player character itself, the character is parented to an object with the code so it's also slightly affected by the code. Because of this, the collider on the player character also registers the triggers and sends them back to the code to adjust the score. This leads to the player losing two points instead of just one point as originally designed. To fix this problem, you just have to turn the box collider off of the player character. The parent of the character has all the code needed and a box collider of their own, so removing the box collider on the character itself just prevents the same thing from happening twice within the game. See Figure 13-3 for an example.

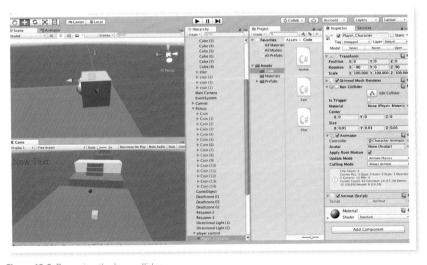

Figure 13-3: Removing the box collider.

THE HEIGHT OF SOME PLATFORMS ARE HIGHER THAN THE CHARACTER CAN JUMP

One of the last problems in the game comes from the level design of the game. This problem didn't come up earlier. Before this, the players actually had the ability to jump higher because there was enough room to give the characters a running start. With the introduction to enemies and environmental hazards, that same jumping power has been limited. Because of this, some of the platforms are too high for the players to actually jump properly.

The fix for this problem is actually really simple: Just add stairs! For the platforms that can't be jumped or have no alternative ways of being accessed, the addition of stairs (see Figure 13-4) doesn't diminish the difficulty of the game. Instead, they improve the game by giving the player the ability to actually progress forward.

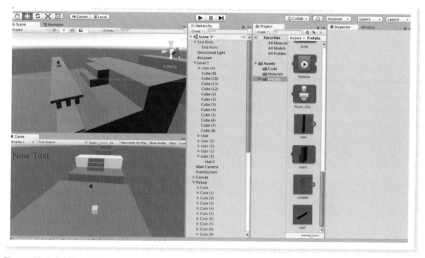

Figure 13-4: Adding stairs.

WRAPPING UP THE NOTICEABLE ISSUES

These are just a handful of the problems that players may experience within the game. As a developer, your job is to listen to any and all of the criticisms and do your best to resolve them. Glitches and bugs happen in games. Even games that have been play tested multiple times have these problems. You'll likely never find *all* the possible bugs in your game, especially the larger and more complex your game gets.

When you can, fix the problems that you notice — but know when to prioritize. Some problems are far more noticeable than others and need to be fixed right away, but other problems hardly effect gameplay at all so you can put them off until later. The problems that affect the way the game plays at its core are what you should fix first because they can interfere with the flow and fun of the game.

REMEMBER

Eventually, you'll have to put the game out there, and no one is ever totally satisfied with what they make. Those who are will never grow because they aren't looking at where they can improve. Strive for perfection while accepting flaws. This doesn't mean you should ignore your mistakes — you just shouldn't be devastated by them.

Take any criticism you get in stride and know that no game is perfect. Strive to make the best game possible, test it, and adjust it to better fit the players you desire, but don't get lost in fixing everything.

14

Finalizing Your Game

In the preceding chapters, you created and refined the first level of your game. Now it's time to put the final touches on the level so that you can create new levels and move beyond just a single-level game.

In this chapter, you'll learn how to code the game to load a new level when it has been finished. You'll also learn how to fix the code so that you can get the character to respawn when they die in the level. Finally, you'll learn how to export your game so that you can play it anytime!

CREATING MULTIPLE LEVELS

You've made one level for your game so far, but games aren't just one level. Most games have multiple levels that players progress through, increasing the difficulty as the levels go on. Your game should be no different. Unity gives you the ability to easily create new levels and connect the levels together in your game.

First, you need to create the new level:

1. **With your first level open, choose File⇨ New Scene.**

   This will create a new empty scene within your overall project.

2. **Save the new scene as Level2, and open your first level again.**

3. **Create a new C# code, and name it Level2 (see Figure 14-1).**

4. **Open the new code.**

5. **At the top of the code, where the code lists all the collections and engines that the code will be using, type the following:**

```
using UnityEngine.SceneManagement;
```

This code will give access to Unity's Scene Manager tool. The Scene Manager allows to control the different scenes using the code. You can use it to load levels and reload levels with a touch of a button or when something is triggered. In this case the Level2 code will be added to the endpoint so that when the player triggers the game object the game will load level 2 on the screen.

REMEMBER

Unity organizes the game in two parts: projects and scenes. The *project* is the overall game that you're making, keeping all the assets and levels organized in one folder. When the game is compiled, you're compiling the project and chosen levels together. *Scenes* are the individual levels in your game. When you create a new scene in the project, the project tracks those scenes and even shares the prefabs, codes, and materials that you've made in other scenes within the new scene.

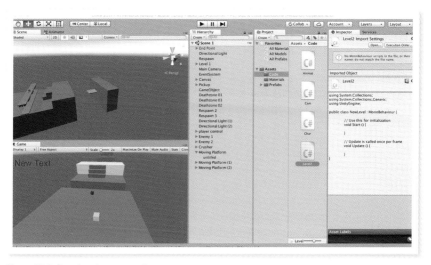

Figure 14-1: Creating the new code.

6. **Delete both the** `void Start` **and** `void Update` **strings.**

They won't be necessary for the code.

7. **In place of the** `void Start` **and** `void Update` **strings, type the following:**

```
void OnTriggerEnter(Collider other) {
```

This will indicate to the code that this string is activated when the collider has a collision with another game object. Inside the code, you'll define what code will be activated when the trigger happens and how it will affect the rest of the game.

REMEMBER

Close off all open brackets. Otherwise, the code won't be able to be properly read by the game.

8. **Inside the** `void` **trigger, type the following code:**

```
if (other.gameObject.CompareTag("Player")) {
```

This will make it so that when the collider touches a game object with the tag `Player`, the code that is within the brackets will happen.

REMEMBER

Be sure to check that your player controller has the tag `Player`.

9. **Add the following code within the** `if` **statement brackets:**

```
Scene.Manager.LoadScene ("Level2");
```

This final bit of code will access the Scene Manager tool and tell it to load the scene titled Level2 that is connected to your game. This code can be used to load any of the other scenes within your project. You can see a completed version of what the code should look like in Figure 14-2.

```
2 using System.Collections.Generic;
3 using UnityEngine;
4 using UnityEngine.SceneManagement;
5
6 public class Level2 : MonoBehaviour {
7
8
9
10      void OnTriggerEnter(Collider other) {
11          if (other.gameObject.CompareTag("Player"))
12          {
13
14              SceneManager.LoadScene("Level2");
15          }
16
17
18      }
19 }
```

Figure 14-2: The new code.

Now if you try to attach this code to your endpoint object, you'll notice that it won't attach. This is because, even though the scenes are within the same project, they aren't actually linked together. Unity doesn't automatically assume that all the scenes within the project folder will be included within the final game. In fact, this ability to pick and choose which levels are built into the game can save you the headache of having to actually move the files out of the project folder. Instead, you can just remove them from the build settings or not even include them in the build settings.

To make it so that scenes can be linked together, follow these steps:

1. **Choose File ⏷ Build Settings.**

   The Build Settings window (shown in Figure 14-3) appears, giving you different options for your game.

Figure 14-3: The Build Settings window.

2. **In the Platform box, select PC, Mac & Linux Standalone.**

   This indicates the type of platform that you want the game to be played on.

3. **From the Target Platform drop-down list, select PC, Mac, or Linux.**

   The target platform is the platform that Unity will format the game for. Unity can make games for all sorts of consoles, such as PS4 and Xbox One, but the controls that you coded the game to will only work on a computer, so you want this to be PC, Mac, or Linux (depending on what computer you're using to build the game and making the game for).

4. **In the Scenes in Build box, select which scenes will be included in the build.**

   To add a new scene, click Add Open Scenes and Unity will automatically include the scene that is open into the build.

After you include Scene 1 in the build, open Level2 from earlier and include it in the build. When both Level2 and Scene 1 are included in the build, the scenes will be linked together and can be called upon by each other.

Now you can attach your Level2 code to the endpoint object. When the player touches the object, the level will automatically switch to level 2. If you test this within Unity, it will automatically open Level2 in Unity.

RESETTING THE LEVEL

Up until this point, when the character dies, the player is destroyed and the game sends a message saying that the player has lost. Instead, you're going to change it so that the game will still present you with a lose screen, but when you press a certain key the game will restart. Follow these steps:

1. **Open your Char code.**

2. **Add the following to the top of the code:**

   ```
   using UnityEngine.SceneManagement;
   ```

   This code alters and controls the scene.

3. **At the end of all the `if` statements, within the `void` trigger string, find the code `if (count <= -1)` and delete that entire section of code, including the code within the `if` statement.**

   Do this for all the `if` statements within the `void` collider.

4. **Where you deleted all that code, write the following:**

```
if (count <= -1) {
winText.text = "You Lose :( Press R to Play Again"
dead = true;
}
```

This code will be within the `void` but on its own so that you don't need to change the code in each of the `if` statements like you had to earlier (see Figure 14-4).

```
165            transform.position = respawnPoint3.transform.position;
166            count = count - 1;
167            SetCountText ();
168
169
170
171     }
172     if (other.gameObject.CompareTag("EnviroHazard 3")) {
173            transform.position = respawnPoint3.transform.position;
174            count = count - 1;
175            SetCountText ();
176     }
177
178     if (count <= -1) {
179            winText.text = "You lose :( (Press R to Play again)";
180            dead = true;
181     }
182 }
183
184     void SetCountText ()
185     {
186     countText.text = "Count: " + count.ToString ();
187
188     }
```

Figure 14-4: Adding the level to the build.

Instead of destroying the game object, you'll use a new Boolean `dead` to affect the gameplay. Right now, `dead = true` has no effect on the game, but that's because you haven't defined `dead` yet. Follow these steps:

1. **At the top of the code, where you keep all the public and private floats, text, and game objects, add the following code:**

```
public bool dead = false;
```

This will give the value of false to the `dead` bool and make it so that the code will recognize the value of the `dead` bool. The goal is to have it so that whenever the player is dead (when the `dead` bool is true), the player won't be able to move or use her character.

2. **Change all the `if` statements in the void FixedUpdate to include the condition that `dead` needs to be false.**

Similar to adding the `sprint` function, simply add at the end of the `if` code `&& dead = = false`. Repeat this for all the `if` statements within the `void FixedUpdate` (see Figure 14-5).

Figure 14-5: Making `dead == false`.

Now, whenever the player is not dead, the character will be able to move around freely, but as soon as the character dies, all the movement controls are unable to be used because you added the condition that the character has to *not* be dead in order to move. The player stops working as soon as the character dies, but how can you turn the player back on once the game "ends"?

You've coded the character to stop working. Now you have to code the reset button. In the losing statement, you've already told the player what key she'll need to press to reset the game, so you'll be coding that function in the code. At the end of the `FixedUpdate` code, but before the raycasting codes, add a new `if` statement:

```
if (Input.GetKey(KeyCode.R) && dead = = true) {
SceneManager.LoadScene(SceneManager.GetActiveScene().
   name);
}
```

This code gives the player the ability to reset the game when the character dies. Like the movement codes, this code only happens when the player presses a certain button on the keyboard — in this case, the R key. And because of the `&& dead = = true` addition, this code won't work unless the player has already died. When the player presses R the Scene Manager will reload the scene from the beginning, which resets the game back to the way it was at the start of the level, so any and all text and counts will be reset to their starting values. Figure 14-6 shows how the code should look.

```
86      {
87          transform.position += Vector3.right * Time.deltaTime * Speed;
88      }
89
90      if (Input.GetKey (KeyCode.Space) && GroundTouch == true && dead == false) {
91          transform.position += Vector3.up * Time.deltaTime * jump;
92          if (directionText.text == "Press Space to Jump") {
93              directionText.text = "Left Shift to Sprint";
94          }
95      }
96      if (Input.GetKey(KeyCode.R) && dead == true) {
97          SceneManager.LoadScene(SceneManager.GetActiveScene().name );
98      }
99
100
101     Vector3 gc = transform.TransformDirection (Vector3.down);
102     Vector3 wc = transform.TransformDirection (Vector3.left);
103
104     if (Physics.Raycast (transform.position, gc, 0.5f)) {
105         GroundTouch = true;
106     }
107
108     if (Physics.Raycast (transform.position, wc, 0.4f)) {
109         transform.position += Vector3.back * Time.deltaTime * wall;
110     }
...
```

Figure 14-6: The reset code.

EXPORTING YOUR GAME

REMEMBER

The game that you've made has been designed with a computer in mind, so make sure that when you export the final build you export with the correct platform.

Now that your game is completed, you need to export the game so that it can be played without Unity. There are two ways to do this:

- You can choose File ⟹ Build.

- You can build the game in the Build Settings window after double-checking to make sure all the settings are correct.

You'll also be able to name the file whatever you want. And when you export the game, you can choose to export it out to a certain location. Exporting it into your games folder will make it easy to find and open, but you don't need to keep it with the project folder because the build is standalone, apart from the project folders and doesn't need to reference them for any of its parts.

When you open the game, you'll see the screen shown in Figure 14-7.

This just gives you the options to open up the game with different screen resolutions and with different qualities. The best combination will vary from computer to computer. The Input tab shows the input controls that the game could use if you used

Figure 14-7: The opening game screen.

Unity's built-in controllers as opposed to the ones that you made on your own in this project.

Open the game and play to make sure that the game is working the way that you programmed it to!

CONTINUING YOUR GAME DESIGN

Now that you've completed the game in this book, try your hand at designing a game on your own. You've learned the tools of Unity and some of the coding that goes into game development. Use the lessons in this book as a guide to creating your own unique games that you can publish and show your friends and family.

This book is just the first step in your game design career! Hopefully, it'll get you to think of game design from the bottom up. As a test, try to make more levels for the game you created in this book with different enemies and objectives. Play around and see how much you can change and make your own in the game.

The most important thing is that you continue to play videogames and ask questions. Think about what you like about games, push yourself to learn more, and create something that is not only fun but special. Make games that are your own and that mean something to you and you'll will find a way to succeed at designing from there. Keep learning and keep designing!

REMEMBER

Have fun!

PATRICK MCCABE is an instructor at the Digital Arts Experience. He has spent the past year teaching students about everything from animation to game design. He graduated from SUNY Purchase in 2016 and studied at three different schools for film and animation. In high school, Patrick won the first-ever award for Best Animation in the Greenwich Youth Film Festival for his short *I Am an Animator.*

He is also a not-so-secret *Star Wars* enthusiast and will not hesitate to tell everyone about it.

DEDICATION

This book is dedicated to my fiancé, Shela, without whom I probably never would have been able to finish. Thank you for always listening when I talked your ears off about random videogames, and for making sure that my glass of Diet Pepsi was always filled.

This book is also dedicated to Diet Pepsi. You were always there to pick me up when I was down. I love you.

AUTHOR'S ACKNOWLEDGMENTS

Thank you to John Wiley & Sons for giving me the opportunity to write this book. This was an amazing experience to write and really challenged me to think through and put to words my feelings on game design and develop a new appreciation for game design itself.

Thank you to Steven Hayes for keeping me on task and emailing me the (many) times I fell behind schedule or was stuck on how I should approach each chapter. I don't think I would have been able to complete this book without you.

Nick, without you I don't think this book would be half as long as it is. I think I came to you about seven different times a day to ask you to help workshop the code when it wasn't working. You are also the father of the curriculum that I used as the basis for this class. Thank you so much for all of the help.

Thank you, Cristina and Jordan, for the shoulders to cry on when I was having trouble motivating myself to write. You two were the heroes I didn't deserve. Cristina, you especially in the last few weeks were like my best book friend. Between our discussions of writing after every Thursday meeting, to the times where we both tried to wrap our heads around our formatting woes, you were the only person who understood the difficulty I had in writing. Honestly, I don't think there was anyone else who could appreciate the pictures of Frodo I sent at the end like you could.

I also have to thank Rob Kissner. It just doesn't seem fair not to. Rob and his company, Digital Arts Experience, are the reason why I was even able to write this book. I remember when Rob asked me to write this book. "Hey, Pat, do you know Unity, and can you write a book on it?" Rob was nothing but encouraging the entire time and whenever I was freaking out about getting the chapters in on time he would just listen with a smile and a joke ready. Rob, there is so much to thank you for, and to say that you are one of the most wonderful people I've ever met would be an understatement. Thank you, Bert, for everything.

Thank you, Shela, for being there for me throughout this entire book and always pretending to be super interested in how the game mechanics of Five Nights at Freddy's create a sense of helplessness in the game to help emphasize the horror of the situation. Shela, you were always there when I needed you most and thank you so much for listening. You are the best partner a guy like me could ever ask for. Between refilling my soda when it was empty to giving me a hug when I'd had a long day writing, everything you did was special and important. There are no words that can describe everything you did for me. You are my best friend in the world, and I love you.

Finally, thank you to Elizabeth Kuball for making me sound smarter than I actually am. You are the reason this book is even remotely readable, and I don't think there are enough words to describe how grateful I am to you for dealing with every delay and problem I've had while writing this book. I am so happy and grateful I was able to work with you to help bring this book into reality.

PUBLISHER'S ACKNOWLEDGMENTS

EXECUTIVE EDITOR: Steven Hayes

PROJECT EDITOR: Elizabeth Kuball

SR. EDITORIAL ASSISTANT: Cherie Case

PRODUCTION EDITOR: Vasanth Koilraj

COVER IMAGE: © FrankRamspott / iStockphoto